Ottakar's LOCAL HISTORY *Series*

Crewe

A scene in Ruskin Road in the early twentieth century.

Ottakar's LOCAL HISTORY *Series*

Crewe

Compiled by
Angela Twiss

OTTAKAR'S

TEMPUS

First published 2001
Copyright © Ottakar's plc, 2001

Ottakar's Local History Series
produced in association with
Tempus Publishing Limited
The Mill, Brimscombe Port,
Stroud, Gloucestershire, GL5 2QG

ISBN 0 7524 2297 9

Typesetting and origination by
Tempus Publishing Limited
Printed in Great Britain by
Midway Colour Print, Wiltshire

Contents

Foreword

In 1837, the young Queen Victoria succeeded to the throne, the book *Oliver Twist* was first published and the Crewe railway station opened. At that time Crewe was a hamlet set in the Cheshire Countryside and was then known as Monks Coppenhall, earning its living through agriculture. The Crewe railway station was located at a point where the Nantwich and Sandbach turnpike road crossed the tracks of the Grand Junction Railway. Passengers from the surrounding areas travelled to Crewe by coach to catch the train, which ran between Birmingham and Newton Junction.

The very first train arrived at Crewe station at 8.45 a.m. on 4 July 1837, and after a stay of eleven minutes it steamed away to Birmingham. The station in those days consisted of a small platform close to the site of the present Crewe Arms Hotel. It is said that the twelve daily trains that passed through the Crewe station were flagged forward by a 'constable'.

In 1842 the Grand Railway Company had moved its engineering company from Liverpool to Crewe. The new railway town soon developed, drawing its expanding workforce from the Midlands, Liverpool and Wales. The first steam locomotive to be built in Crewe was completed in 1845 and was named *Columbine*, a 2-2-2 locomotive whose working life had lasted until 1902.

By the end of Victoria's reign in 1901, the population of Crewe had risen to over 30,000 and the Crewe station had established itself as the hub of the railway network.

Between 1903 and 1906, Crewe station had been extended for a third time, an island platform had been added and tunnel lines had been laid to enable freight trains to bypass the station.

On Monday 21 April 1913, on the eve of the Great War, King George V and Queen Mary visited Crewe Works which then employed 7,000 men in the locomotive works and several thousand more in the station, engine sheds and shunting yards.

At the outbreak of the Second World War, the main line traffic was mostly operated by steam locomotives. All the major stations and railway facilities were geared to the steam age.

After the war the main junctions such as Crewe, and the engines it produced, had been well used and the diesel locomotive was already a viable prospect for the future.

By the early 1950s Crewe had a population of 60,000, of whom 10,000 were employed by British Railways. Crewe station was again in full swing, with 9,000 passengers starting or terminating their journeys at Crewe each week.

In the 1960s and '70s the steam locomotives went out of service, and the railway network was cut back as the competition from road and air transport intensified.

By the 1980s Crewe station had reached the limit of its operational efficiency with its existing equipment, and in 1983 British Rail decided to invest £14.3 million in a complete resignalling and track remodelling programme at Crewe, and the station was shut down for a period of seven weeks so that the intensive engineering work could be carried out.

The shutdown period between 2 June and 21 July 1985 was timed to take advantage of the summer weather and the maximum daylight hours, with engineering teams working around the

Just passing through. Sir John Mills before his knighthood, in the bar at Crewe station in the 1970s.

clock. During this time the Area Manager and his staff made arrangements to ensure that the main line service through Crewe operated normally via independent lines bypassing the station. Local passengers were catered for by rail shuttle services and special bus services to and from Crewe, and part of the railway car park was turned into a bus station for seven weeks!

By careful planning and concentrating the work into a seven-week period, disruption was kept to a minimum and almost £1 million was saved. But for the seven-week shutdown the engineering work would probably have taken four years.

This short history of Crewe railway explains the foundation of how Crewe has grown as a railway town.

The hardship that many families went through during the war years seemed to be overpowered by their unity and their sense of humour. The pleasure of a walk through Crewe Park, a visit to the Kino or Grand cinemas or just a singsong in the Parlour was enough entertainment for most. Children played games of hopscotch, skipping and tic.

When the slum clearance programme was started in the 1960s in Sandbach Street, Stafford Street, Dewes Street, to name but a few, new housing estates were built.

Many people were re-housed in buildings with electricity, gas, gardens, bathrooms – some things that had to be better than gas mantles, flat irons and toilets that were at the bottom of the yard!

Yet Crewe people remember all these bygone years with great affection, 'In the old days times were hard, but we were happy!' Maybe, because there was so little to go around, they never expected very much, and because of the war they were made to sit night after night in air-raid shelters talking to each other. Everybody knew each other's needs and were willing to help

In the twenty-first century Crewe has changed enormously. Old buildings have disappeared and been replaced by new estates and roads. Many new families have moved into the area as large industrial estates have increased employment. Yet there are many people, whose families go back generations, still working for the Railway Works, Rolls-Royce or local companies, who have nostalgic recollections of their town.

Crewe Square in 1952.

Introduction

It was with some excitement that Ottakar's started out on a venture that became known as the Local History Project, an attempt to uncover the past in Crewe from a variety of different viewpoints. Recording history now will help future generations to understand the past present and future of Crewe and its surrounding villages.

The Local History Project asked people to send in articles – either their own memories or researched pieces of local history – with the best ones being published in this book. The response was very impressive, both in terms of the quality and the passion with which people participated. I believe that we have been able to create a unique document, chronicling Crewe in a way that has never been done before.

Included in this collection are recollections on many aspects of life in Crewe, including childhood, the war years, local businesses, buildings and family life, and times many still call 'the good old days'.

What has become obvious in editing this book is that Crewe is an area rich in local history, with a heritage that deserves to be recorded. From the formally researched history of Bunbury, to the wonderfully anecdotal memories of Mabel Parker, these form the bedrock of the past that makes Crewe what it is today.

In the Acknowledgements I have thanked many individuals by name. Here I would like to add my general thanks to everyone who has shown an interest in this project. It has been a pleasure to put this book together, and often the hardest decision has been to decide what must be left out. I hope you get as much pleasure in discovering the past in *Crewe* as I have editing it.

Angela Twiss
August 2001

Acknowledgements

Gerald Elson, Phyllis Green, Dee Reynolds, Nora Schofield, Michael Robinson, Rhonwen Saunders, Mabel Parker, Gareth Roberts, Joan Bebbington, W.L. Wright, Ted Tunstall, George Ingham, Evan Williams, Nigel Ansell Roberts, J.E. Elsworth, Kathleen Armstrong, Colin McLean, Charles Parker, Joseph Jeffrey Tudor, R.J. Davies, D.A. Baker, Roy Butler, Godfrey Brown, Ken Parton and everyone who was not successful in having their story published but took the time and effort to write a piece for the Local History Project. To all of you I give a sincere thank-you! I would also like to thank Brian Edge who helped me with a few ideas on the layout, Howard Curran, our local historian, who helped with the extremely difficult choice of selecting three winning entries, and special thanks to Dave Fox, Editor of the *Crewe Chronicle*, for also helping to select the winning entries and for his continuing support in getting this project up and running.

I would especially like to thank my dad Gordon for his help and expertise, my husband Ivor, and children, Andrew and Nicola for putting up with me while I have hidden myself away in front of the computer for many nights!

CHAPTER 1
The War Years

How the bombed dairy looked from the front in Ruskin Road.

The Night My Grandma's House Was Bombed

I suppose the date of 26 September 1940 holds very little significance for the vast majority of Crewe residents. However, for my Grandma and her family that date would be etched in their memories forever. The evening of 26 September 1940 was when her house had a direct 'hit' by a high explosive German bomb. It appears that a string of bombs that night landed on the south side of Crewe causing some structural damage but by far the worst being inflicted on Callwood's dairy and Grandma's home.

My maternal grandmother had lived behind Callwood's dairy at No. 71 Ruskin Road for a couple of years before the incident. Having been a widow since 1933, she resided there with her two youngest children, George and Mabel. George was employed in the railway works and was working regular nights. Mabel, whose husband was in the army, had a younger daughter Pat, and all three lived with Grandma. On this fateful night George was going to work as usual for 8 p.m. while Mabel had decided to take her daughter to visit her in-laws at Colwyn Bay. To save Grandma being in the house on her own, she had decided to spend the night with her eldest daughter Doris (my mother) in Wistaston Road.

She left her home at around 7 p.m. that night with George on his way to work. Mr Callwood, the dairy owner, was just closing the shop and said to Grandma, 'Where are you going to, Mrs Bull?' She replied, 'Because of the air raids I'm going to my daughter's.' 'Jump in the car – I'll run you down there.' I'm sure as my Grandma got into his car she never in her wildest dreams

realized that this was the last night she would ever see her home.

I'm told the air-raid sirens sounded quite early that night – even before George got to work. Of course when the sirens sounded there was the usual scramble to find the right shelter. There were a number where I lived with my parents in Wistaston Road. There were two brick ones built in Lewis Street and another by the side of the Hop Pole public house in Wistaston Road. Residents of that area also used the freshly converted one under Flag Lane baths. Many private shelters, ranging from the Anderson shelters in some people's gardens to converted cellars, supplemented the public ones. All these different types of shelters were where the locals would spend many nights in the early years of the war. Before going into the shelter certain formalities had to take place with a strict ritual being followed. Everyone, without exception, took their gas masks with them as well as their identity cards, clothing and ration books. This was to ensure that if your home (like Grandma's) was bombed, you had at least the bare essentials to survive with you.

When the sirens sounded that night, my parents, Grandmother and myself were invited to hurry down to next door's cellar. This was the home of Mr Carroll, a highly respected local cobbler, whose business was in High Street. The cellar, if memory serves me right, had recently been strengthened with corrugated roofing and cast-iron supports bolted to the floor and ceiling. However, it was quite comfortable having had electric lighting installed. Quite unusual when most shelters (except the baths) had no lighting at all. There were chairs for everyone to sit on. In fact there was a three-piece suite, very comfortable to

This view from Lunt Avenue shows the devastation of the dairy. The houses opposite have had their windows blown out and slates blown off the roof.

while away the hours until the all-clear siren sounded.

Everyone was convinced that being down the cellar was just a formality. Only larger towns and cities would be bombed. Nothing like that would ever happen in Crewe. In that cellar that night, myth became a reality and some of the horrors of war were brought home. I can remember quite vividly how everyone's expressions changed quite dramatically when suddenly from the calm of an autumn evening the thud of bombs falling could be clearly felt. The cellar shook quite violently; everyone in there was absolutely convinced Wistaston Road was taking direct hits. We later learned this was not so. The nearest bomb was dropped on Alton Street, which

was about half a mile from Mr Carroll's cellar.

It was about 10.30 p.m. when the ARP visited my grandmother in the shelter explaining that her home had taken a direct hit but she couldn't go until morning to inspect it. They were concerned to know if anybody was at home but Grandma was able to allay their fears. She was able to tell them George was on nights in the Works whilst her daughter and grand-daughter were away in North Wales.

The next morning, 27 September 1940, was without doubt one of the biggest shocks my mother, grandmother and I would ever experience. Grandmother's home and the dairy were nothing but a pile of rubble. Grandma's neat home had been reduced, by

Sydney Jones, Gilbert's brother, in his Liverpool Constabulary Uniform before he joined up as a soldier in the King's Liverpool Regiment, where he fell at Ypres on 24 October 1917.

a high explosive bomb, to a shattered and totally destroyed shell. Her furniture along with many personal items had all gone in the flick of an eyelid. The curtains fluttered in the breeze through the remains of the broken windows. The one item that had survived that night was her granddaughter's pram. It was still situated under the stairs where it had been left, covered in dust but without any real damage to it.

Her friends and neighbours of the area were full of remorse and sympathy for what had happened. Most were genuinely concerned and offered what little help they could, helping her gather from the rubble what little had survived that night's bombing. This was a new experience for everyone and no one was quite sure how to deal with it. However, irrespective of what had happened, Grandma and her family were quite resilient, knowing full well it could never be the same; but life would go on.

Although some bombing had taken place a few days earlier on railway land, inflicting some minor damage, as far as I can establish Grandma's home was the first civilian property in Crewe to be totally destroyed by enemy action during the Second World War. Grandma's home had been wiped out but fortunately no casualties had been taken. That was not the case in future bombings, as the next twelve months in the town's history would bear witness.

Howard Curran

Working in Crewe

My late father Gilbert Jones was one of nine children born to William and Miriam Jones, who lived at Bedford Street, Crewe. William was a telegraphist at Crewe station. Now seventy, I'm the elder of his two sons.

Their children were Noel, Seymour, Gertrude, Miriam, Catherine, Fred, Sydney, Gilbert and Cecil. Sydney was in the Liverpool constabulary before the war, then joined up and as a soldier of the King's Liverpool Regiment subsequently fell at Ypres on 24 October 1917, aged twenty-six. He is buried at Solferino Farm cemetery in Belgium.

A happy outcome of our sons researching Sydney's life and death resulted in them finding out where he had lived before his death in Edleston Road, Crewe, and from this we were able to find that his granddaughter, Cheryl Jones was alive and living in Crewe. She had thought she was the last remaining Jones descended from William and Miriam, and has been delighted to find a thriving tribe of relatives in Oxfordshire!

Gilbert Jones wrote the following notes for an autobiography in 1981, when he was seventy-nine. He was already very ill with cancer and died in 1984 without completing the biography. He had emigrated to Canada after the Second World War and ultimately took Canadian citizenship, marrying a Canadian lady as his second wife.

Crewe Boy

I hope there are a few old Crewe folks who remember the early days in the wonderful town of Crewe and, now at nearly eighty years old, I would like to relate to young and old life as it was to this Crewe lad in the hard times before and after the 1914 war, a picture of those energetic people, skilful in all trades and professions, who worked long hours – which was then the tradition – 6 a.m. to 5.30 p.m., accepted without question. I want to describe what life was like then, when work conditions were not the best and there was little money for one's labour. But first, I want the folks of Crewe to be proud of their past achievements and contributions to the country. They produced inventions never heard of in the news and, as I get older, my admiration for those Crewites is beyond praise.

I hope today's generation of young people can picture life in 1912 when, for my first job as a lather boy, I was rubbing chins in a barber shop, I think the name was Grocott, next to Galloway chemists, Nantwich Road and Mill Street, 8 a.m. to 10 p.m. for a shilling wage. Sometimes it wasn't pleasant to rub a drunk's face, late in the day and being very tired, slipping a little soap into his mouth and bringing out a stream of vulgarity, which at that age I didn't savvy. Having a musical ear, my attention was wandering, listening to the organ grinder outside the shop playing *Alexander's Ragtime Band*.

I played football for the Bedford Street school team, 1912 league. I joined the scouts, Bedford Street second troop, joined the bugle band and practised regularly. Our Scoutmaster was Mr Pincombe, a fine man who was a bridge designer for the LNW Railway. He took us to camp frequently at Trickett's farm, Rope Lane. Both his wife and daughter Kathleen came on these camps, and Mr Trickett the farmer was very helpful to us all. With a scout friend I decided to take a holiday for two weeks at my uncle's farm at Longport, Staffs, so my scout friend, Frank Goodwin from the school (a very clever boy) and I took a handcart with

tent and food and trekked from Crewe to Longport, 24 miles.

The first night's camp was uneventful, but the second was spoiled by part-time boys from the nearby colliery, Parkhouse Pit, who let the tent down in the early morning. The second day I was ready for them, having borrowed my uncle's air rifle, an old German gun and very powerful. When the tent went down and the lads ran away I picked the nearest one and shot him in the bottom. His arms went up and he ran even faster. I'd made my mark, but after this incident my uncle took back his air gun, as the lad I'd shot had been taken to the doctor to have the pellet removed from his backside. With no more interference from the miner lads, Frank and I had a very pleasant holiday, then the trek home, a wonderful time.

My second job was a very pleasant one, but didn't last above a month. This was as an errand boy for two ladies who kept a cake shop, and it was my duty to carry out baskets of pork pies from Crewe to a shop in Willaston. I had to travel over the fields, and the smell of the pies was so appetising I was tempted to make a small hole in the top of a pie and suck out the juice from within without damaging the pie. After a few excursions someone saw me in the act in the field, one basket at each side, and reported me to the ladies' bakery – hence I was fired.

At this time there was no motorised transit system in Crewe, but horse-cabs lined up forty strong outside the station. There were also Wards House Buses stagecoaches, which carried twelve people. A later competitor was a man named Gregory, who introduced a 25-steam charabanc. This was successful, so the Railway bought two petrol buses, called 'Greyhounds', which put Mr Gregory out of business. I remember and admire him for the

Gilbert Jones in Toronto, Ontario, Canada May in 1959.

service he provided when a walk to the market and back from Bedford Street on a dirty night was no picnic. One thing I enjoyed on a winter's night at the market was a penny black-pudding, hot, with mustard – wow! It somehow tasted better with the smell of the burning oil lamps.

Life was hard, but everyone accepted it. Crewe was a work town and the largest rail centre in England, although I never hear it being mentioned today. In my opinion the great park was one of the best in England, although the long walk past the Alton Street – Wistaston Road Gas Works was none too pleasant. The main streets were Nantwich Road, Mill Street, Edleston Road, Exchange Street, Market Street, Victoria Street, Hightown and High Street. On Saturday afternoons boys would gather near the LNW station to collect engine names and numbers. Some may remember Blind Teddy, with his little dog and the tin cup he would shake to passers-by at the station. This I could not understand, that a blind man had to rely on handouts when certain folks had many. This was the system when England owned half the world.

During the 1914-18 War we Boy Scouts did play a part, helping wounded soldiers when they arrived by train in Crewe. We soon got used to the sight of blood and terrible injuries. Soldiers had been in the trenches with no change of clothing or socks and were lousy, so it was our job, which we relished, to carry their rifles and gear to the Soldiers' Rest, just outside Crewe station, where they were deloused and given clean underwear before going home for a week to stay with their families. We felt very important, and we were rewarded by soldiers who gave us badges, buttons and empty cartridge cases.

A boy named Booth, I think the son of a family who owned a chemist business, carried me on the handlebars of his bike going to the Soldiers' Rest for duty. Passing Mill Street, he looked around at a policeman, took his mind off his steering and ran me straight into a pony and trap. The bike was demolished but we were luckily uninjured.

At fourteen I got a job at a large clothing factory, Doody's, and made a few extra pennies being a model for boys' clothing. I worked on the third floor in the despatch department, running up and down six flights of stairs. Sometimes I had to bring up large baskets used for packing clothes and deliver to other floors on a lift which had only two sides, one open to the street, the other to the interior of the building. Sitting on an empty basket, I overbalanced and fell between the street opening and the wall, from the first floor to the ground floor. I dropped 10ft and landed on my head in the bottom of the lift well. I was unconscious for a while, but the factory gave me two weeks holiday with pay. That is how accidents were settled then.

I next got a job on the LMS despatch at Forge Street, working in a little office as general messenger boy, and driving a crane in the yard after one day's tuition. I had to be up at 5 a.m. to be at work at 6 a.m., and in the dark winter mornings I ran all the way, two miles, to Forge Street, scared of the dark, carrying my lunch and tea can. If you were one minute late you were locked out until 9 a.m. My wage for that job was 4s 6d a week.

At fourteen and a half I left the LMS despatch and secured a seven-year apprenticeship to make electrical instruments at Gresty Road electric shops. The foreman, Mr H. Hately, lived next door to us. This was an interesting job and I was soon being shown how to operate different machines which I was very interested in. One very cold morning, after starting at 6 a.m., I found a nice spot on a large heating oven used for drying armatures, so taking advantage of the absence of the big boss, I snuggled down on top of it for forty winks. Alas, after twenty minutes of glorious sleep I was awakened surrounded by workmen who revived me with a can of cold water, so sleeping on the oven in future was out.

As railway employees we could get quarter fares, so some other apprentices and I decided to buy a bell tent and camp out at Beeston Castle, as we could get a train every morning to take us to work. This was the old scouting routine, which was very handy and useful in a hundred ways. We were four strong and all friends, so we decided that when the autumn came in we would camp the winter, build a shack and acquire a large old stove to heat it. This we did, and with heat and four bunks we weathered three winters, and never went short of vegetable and rabbit, all free for the taking.

Water was no problem, as we found a spring on the hillside and we piped it in and the water was really cold. One day the farmer, passing, asked how we managed without water to drink, so we showed him our spring water pipe. He had a big laugh and told us where it came from – his cow shippon – but after draining 250 yards through sand it was always clear, and after drinking it for so long no ill effects were recorded.

In 1916 King George V visited Crewe Works, and the Boy Scouts stood as guard of honour, 200 of us lined up on a very cold day for the arrival of His Majesty. Two hours later he came, and we were perished. He raised his hand as his car passed by without a cheer. To compensate for the wait, we were given a large coffee at the Crewe Arms Hotel.

In 1917 my brother, Sydney Harry Jones, was killed in France. This was a very sad day for all at home, and although at that time I didn't fully understand the war, I could have killed a hundred soldiers to avenge my brother, given the opportunity.

Gilbert Jones

War On The Buses

I was lying face down under the canteen table in the Crosville Bus Depot, when the German bombs I had heard whistling down moments before came a bit too close for comfort and began to explode around me. To think that I had volunteered for war work on the buses so that if the German bombers came for me I would have a chance of running! I had had the chance of working at Rolls Royce but never went to the interview. No sitting targets for me! Instead I volunteered as a bus conductress, a chance to help the war effort in the open.

I had, on this particular day, been first off-shift and was waiting at the depot at the top of Queen Street when the whistling sound started. I dived under the table. The explosion lifted me bodily off the floor and dropped me again. When I got up and opened the doors of the garage, it was obvious that a bomb had hit the far end. Not one bus had any windows left. There was so much debris that we had to carry our bikes out. Strangely there was clothing hanging from the telegraph wires and rubbish right down to Boots corner in the middle of town. It seemed that the first bomb had completely demolished a house in Earle Street, killing its occupants.

I had been twenty-two when war had been declared and I lived then at the shop in Millstone Lane, Nantwich with Dad and his wife whom he had recently married after Mum had died. It was expected that the single women like me would go to work in the war effort. The buses then seemed a sensible idea but I was not to know that my war on the buses was to be far from uneventful!

Back then very few people owned cars or were able to run the few that there were. If you didn't walk or catch the bus you used a bike. So one of the biggest drawbacks of working on the buses was that I had to get from Nantwich to Crewe for the start of the early shift which began at 4.15 a.m. I used to bike the five miles in the dark, and very lonely it was too. Coming off shift was not as bad since I used to join groups of other cyclists whose work finished about the same time, and cycled with them to Willaston and beyond. The early shift ended about 1.30 p.m. but the late shift finished well after midnight.

The buses were important to the war effort in Crewe. They were the chief means of transporting workers to and from Rolls Royce and the railway works, schedules and routines were set to make sure that the workers got to work and home on time. But it was work not made particularly easy by the problems created by the weather, the

Mabel Parker at the outbreak of war in 1939, aged twenty-two. Just as in the First World War, young ladies were required to volunteer for work that in peacetime they would have not have contemplated. In those days young women who were married had been expected to stay at home. The war changed all that.

bombing, the buses themselves, sabotage and even the travelling public.

Nowadays, a frost warning is enough to get the gritters out. Not then. With so little traffic and no attempt made to clear the roads, snow and ice were perpetual hazards for our overcrowded and unstable buses.

I remember once, on the Underwood Lane-Station run, we were stuck in the snow, stopped half way up the bank at Newcastle Street bus stop. I went up the alley to one of the houses, borrowed their dustbin and emptied the ashes under the wheels of the bus. Lo and behold we were on the move again!

On another winter's day we were on the Station-West End run. The driver I had that day was Mr Hockenhull. Instead of turning into Minshull New Road, he went straight on. I rang the bell and he stopped. I went round to the front and told him he'd gone wrong. He explained that the solid snow was too dangerous to reverse on, so he turned into Hulme Street and on to Minshull New Road. In Hulme Street the residents had cleared the snow from the footpaths onto the road, where it had frozen into hard lumps, making it very uneven. The bus skidded and Mr Hockenhull must have hit the accelerator instead of the brake, because the bus took off and shot into the front of a house. I remember flying forward on my knees. With bricks falling all around the drivers cab, the passengers made a quick exit. When I finally got up there were feet marks all down the back of my uniform! No one waited to see if we were all right. Mr Hockenhull had to wait while the house was shored up around him before the bus was finally dragged out!

Once a rather large lady had waited in the snow for us to pick her up at Moorfields in Willaston. In those days you got on the bus

Mabel Parker in 1941. Notice the smart uniform-standards of dress were maintained on the buses throughout the war.

at the back, pulling yourself up onto the rear platform by a vertical bar put there for the purpose. As the large lady pulled herself up, the bus slid slowly to the kerb. She immediately said, 'I didn't do it! I know I'm big but I couldn't pull a bus!'

We do not seem to have pea-soup fogs nowadays, but we had them in the war years! Bus headlights were useless and under blackout regulations they were covered and were only allowed to show two narrow slits of light. Buses were vital though and there was no question of them being withdrawn just because the roads were icy or visibility was nil. One very foggy night we had to take

War on the buses; the front line troops, Queen Street Depot. Opposite side of the road from the bombed garage and canteen.

workers back to Sandbach. The fog was too thick for normal travel, so I led the way on my bike!

In order to confuse the enemy during an air raid on Crewe Works or Rolls Royce they used to light oil barrels along Victoria Avenue. The thick black smoke might have done the trick though. Bus drivers couldn't see their hands in front of their faces and it was just about impossible to see the stops, especially in the hours of darkness. Pollution wasn't such a big issue in those days!

After the damage to the buses in the bombing of the depot, old ones were brought in from Wallasey and Manchester. Wallasey buses were taller and narrower than our own. Care had to be taken when negotiating Mill Street Bridge, as there was only about 5 or 6ins clearance. One day, one of the Wallasey buses had dropped off the workers at Rolls Royce. The driver decided to take a short-cut back to the depot in Queens Street. He headed under the Cumberland Bridge. Whoops! The top half finished up on one side of the bridge, the bottom on the other!

The buses were always full during the war years. There would be an almighty scramble to get on. I had to count the number of passengers going onto the top deck, then stand on the bottom step and shove everyone else inside – 'move along the bus please!' I then had to put a chain across the entrance to ensure no one fell off, and that no one else could get on. Often people unable to get on the bus hung onto the chain, a dangerous thing to do. I often had to smack them across the knuckles with my ticket machine to get them to let go. Imagine doing that nowadays! But there were no complaints, no court actions and no compensation in those days!

After the war was over things began to return to normal. I left the buses in 1946 after my husband, whom I married in 1940 and who had been abroad in the army for three years, came back and settled into work.

Mabel Parker
Prize Winner

A Short History of the Railway Volunteers

In 1887, largely due to the efforts of the Locomotive Superintendent Frank Webb, an entire Corps of Royal Engineers was raised, called the 2nd Cheshire Royal Engineers (Railway) Volunteer Corps,

10th Company, 2nd Cheshire Royal Engineers on their arrival at Cape Town in October 1899. Note the child in the straw hat!

Volunteer Engineers practise track-laying at Rhyl in 1889. Skills such as this and bridge-building were in demand in the South African campaign due to the vast distances involved and the reliance on locomotive transport.

comprising six companies each totalling 100 soldiers (or sappers, as Royal Engineer private soldiers are called).

When the magnificent Queen's Park was opened in July 1888 (where the monument to the Volunteers now stands), the Commander in Chief of the British Army, the Duke of Cambridge, inspected the entire Corps on parade. The Corps had the use of a rifle range under Holmes Chapel viaduct. They conducted track and bridge laying exercises in the dunes along the seafront at Rhyl, where they spent several training weeks. At the time, they were the only reserve military unit in the British Army, perhaps even in the world, who were drawn exclusively from a single employer at a single location, despite claims to the

contrary by an American corps in the 1920s.

In October 1899 Britain was at war with the Boers. In response to rising tension, there were already large numbers of British and colonial troops in South Africa, but further reinforcements were mobilised at home. As the key to fighting a successful campaign across the vast and empty veldts of South Africa would be transport, mobility and logistics, the Railway Volunteers of Crewe received their call. Their special skills would be badly needed by the huge numbers of soldiers already in theatre, and by those preparing to go. As the war progressed, the railways became major arteries serving the outlying towns and garrisons, and many major battles took place within a few miles of the main lines. All

The 2nd Cheshire Royal Engineers march off to war down High Street, Crewe, on 16 October 1899.

three of the main sieges took place in towns with railway stations.

The Railway Volunteers lost ten men in the conflict, from a total of twenty-six men from various regiments who originated in the Crewe area. Nineteen of these men died of disease, three by accidents, and just four were killed by the Boers. Among those who died was Lt C.M.F. Trotter. He was killed at Chatham after being thrown from his horse on 11 April 1901. Sapper Septimus

Robinson perished from enteric (typhoid) fever in the Orange Free State capital of Bloemfontein on 27 May 1900, falling victim to the epidemic that swept through the British troops. Sapper Robinson, originally from Nannerch in North Wales, is buried at the President Brand Garden of Remembrance, Bloemfontein, Republic of South Africa. The names of those who died, along with those of their surviving comrades and other local men who served in South

Crewe station, Number 2 Platform, 1899.

Africa with different units, appear on the magnificent memorial that was erected in Crewe's Queens Park in 1903. There is also a stunning bronze plaque. Originally mounted in St Paul's church on West Street, now resident in the Municipal Buildings, which lists ten of the war dead and also features the Engineer's crest of a shield, crossed tools and scroll, surmounted by a locomotive (a detail of which featured on the uniform collar dogs).

After the demobilisation of the unit in 1902, they continued to train and soldier until 17 March 1912, when they held their final parades in the company of the veterans of the Boer War (some of them still serving in the unit), in the town square and, appropriately, inside Crewe Works itself. The unit was then amalgamated into the newly formed Territorial Army. In 1935, the veterans of the South African campaign were photographed at their reunion in front of the memorial to their service in the Queen's Park. The photograph contains evidence of the mysterious 'Sapper Poppie', a lady who appears in full military dress on a previous photograph from 1897, but who cannot be found on any documentation dating from the period. Her identity, and how she came to be the sole lady in an all-male unit, remains unknown.

The Boer War was one of the first 'media campaigns' where photography and telephony allowed war correspondents (of which Winston Churchill was one) to deliver battlefield reports in a relatively short space of time to the newspapers back in England. A great deal of material has survived but the Boer War remains Britain's 'forgotten war', a dirty little campaign carried out with dubious, if not outright morally unjustifiable, intent, and historically overshadowed by the mass slaughter and horrors of the First World War some years later. It is generally held to be true that lessons were learnt regarding twentieth-century warfare in the Boer War that provided the British Army with a strategic 'headstart' on the Germans in World War One. Given the enormous losses suffered in the event, one wonders what might have been the outcome if this had not been the case.

The Railway Volunteers deserve recognition and remembrance for their service. Their memorial in Queen's Park had a single poppy taped to it last year in the week after Remembrance Sunday. It is heartening to know that someone, at least, has not forgotten.

Noel K. Hannan

CHAPTER 2

Childhood

Children's corner, Valley Park Playground, Crewe.

Flag Lane Bridge and Flag Lane before Crewe baths were built. The baths were opened on 7 November 1923 by the Mayoress of Crewe, Mrs J.R. Goulden.

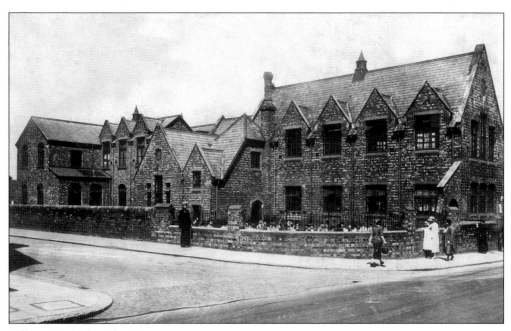

Edleston Road Schools, Crewe.

Some of the boys from Edleston Road Infants School around 1937. From left to right: Raymond Glover, Derek Vickerman, Ronnie Cotterill, Cyril Blount, Colin McLean, Maurice Hazeldene and John Bedson.

A Boy's Eye View

During the war I lived in Alton Street, overlooking the children's playground, where it was not easy to get to sleep on light nights, while others were noisily enjoying themselves.

That side of the road was lined with oil burners to provide a smoke screen on clear moonlit nights to foil German air-raiders. Naturally the sooty smoke which found its way into the house was not popular with my mother. Near the opposite corner of Flag Lane was a communal brick air-raid shelter with a concrete slab roof, but we never used that, as we had our own shelter in the back-yard.

During the worst of the air raids we slept in the shelter on bunks made with a wooden frame covered with wire netting. At other times, particularly in the worst weather, we slept inside under a heavy table, or under the staircase.

To a youngster it was like being kept in on bonfire night, although I was once allowed to look out and see the sky lit up over Flag Lane Bridge as Merseyside burnt.

Going to school, it was a matter of ones

satchel over the shoulder and a cardboard box hanging with a string, hanging over the other, holding a gas mask. Initially I went to Edleston Road School. There we had to practise evacuating the school and going into air-raid shelters which had been constructed out of wood and earth on nearby open space. There we had to practise using our gas masks. I remember being the object of amusement after one such event. The carbon, which was supposed to absorb any gas, had leaked all over my face. I was sent to the headmaster for a replacement.

Craft lessons were largely of a practical nature, we made covers for ration books and identity cards. Our education was not only interrupted by sleepless nights, but indirectly, when the heating system broke down as well. It was not easy to get repairs carried out and for a while we went to school in shifts in the few classrooms which were heated with electric fires mounted high on the walls.

We did not know whether to believe it when other children said that the Germans had invaded Denmark and Norway. We were no doubt more patriotic at that time because we were all taken out of school to line Edleston Road when the King and Queen visited Crewe. They were on their way to visit Rolls Royce to inspect the place

SECONDARY SCHOOL, CREWE. (14)

Ruskin Road, Secondary School, Crewe in 1934.

where the famous Merlin aero-engine was being manufactured.

While this was going on we had to study for the eleven-plus examinations. I moved to what was then the Grammar School in Ruskin Road, where the air-raid shelters had been constructed on the school field. These restricted the area for games. A strip was left around the edge. Here the grass was left to grow and at one time was cut to form a haystack. In winter the field was grazed by sheep. There were green patches, on the otherwise frost-covered grass where they had slept.

Net curtaining was stuck on the windows to prevent injuries by flying glass from bomb blast, and blackout curtains were provided which required an elaborate system for the glass-roofed hall.

Presumably to instill some patriotism we were entertained one day by a piano recital by a Polish refugee, with a bloodstained Polish flag draped over the piano.

The staff and sixth formers took on firewatching duties in case of incendiary bombs. Typically not everything that went on was very serious and there were rumours of soap being stuffed up the spout of the communal staff teapot and of one girl getting daubed with ink. The school railings were removed to provide metal for armament manufacture.

The war also had its effects outside school and air-raid shelters were interesting both out of curiosity and playgrounds. Then at times we went to see the latest bomb damage.

The barrage balloon sites on various pieces of spare ground and Queens Park were also places of interest to youngsters.

However it was not all free time as we were often pressed into having to queue at shops for the meagre rations. This was rather puzzling as with less to buy one would not expect to have longer to wait, except possibly for the delay while the coupons were cut from the ration books. For many of our age group the war came to an end about the time we were leaving school. As a relief from the war and to celebrate victory, loud speakers were mounted on the building of Marks and Spencer and there was dancing on Crewe Square.

Colin McLean

A *True Crewe'ite!*

It is said that to be a true Cockney you have to be born within the sound of Bow Bells.

Likewise, to be a true Crewe'ite. you have to be born within the sound of Christ Church Bells.

Well, I can lay claim to being a true Crewe'ite, as I was born in the centre of town on the corner of Sandbach Street and Delamere Street before it was demolished to make way for the new Queensway.

My mother used to tell me that I was born on a Friday evening just as the Crewe works' buzzer was sounding at half-past-five, so it was inevitable that I should eventually become an apprentice and tradesman in the Loco works.

My home was a typical railway two up and two down cottage: living room and kitchen downstairs, two bedrooms and a small cupboard upstairs, over the porch. It was fitted with an outside loo, which was one of the old tip-pan types. All the wastewater from the house and the rainwater used to run into a container and when it was full it used to tip over and flush away all the contents of the loo. Very cold

A view of Edleston Road from the school in 1958.

in the winter and a bit smelly in the summer, so we used to run the water down the sink until the pan tipped in hot weather.

The houses had solid front doors with a big glass knob in the centre. I remember some of the lads used to get a long piece of string and tie the knobs together, then knock hard on both doors and watch as the occupants tried to open the doors. Harmless fun in those days, but if you were caught you usually ended up with a sore head. The houses were not very big but I feel that an atmosphere was present in these terraced houses, which is sadly missed in today's society. If for any reason one of the neighbours' wives were taken ill, there was no question of the man of the house staying at home from work to look after the children. The rule in those days was no work, no money. So the other families in the street would rally round, take the children in and look after them until the wife was well enough to return to normal life. All this without thought of repayment.

33

My childhood was spent around the town centre. One of my greatest pleasures was the market on a Friday night. It used to be open until well after ten o'clock. No electric lights on the stalls in those days. Tilly pressure lamps that hung on hooks lighted them. I used to stand and watch quacks (unqualified doctors) selling patent medicines, stalls laid out with all kinds of surgical instruments, bottles with long tape worms in them suspended in some kind of liquid. You can imagine what effect this had on a young boy of eleven years. I used to like watching 'Cardy Humbug' making his humbug toffee on a big hook at the side of the stall. Pulling and stretching, then throwing it back over the hook and repeating the procedure all over again, until finally rolling it out and cutting it into small pieces to sell.

There used to be a man selling pottery too. On one occasion he held a set of dinner plates on his arm and because nobody would buy them he threw the lot on the floor smashing all of them, saying that if they wouldn't pay his price then no bugger was having them! This was free entertainment for me.

Living so close to the square, I was able to watch the building of the Odeon cinema by

Wistaston Mill, Crewe, before it became a private house.

Fletcher of Delemere Street. There was a grand opening in 1937, local dignitaries were invited, it was packed with people, the likes of me had no chance of getting in. I remember they were showing a film called *Dark Journey* with Conrad Vielt taking the lead role. There was a commissionaire, Mr Norbury I think his name was. He stood outside shouting the prices of admission something like this, 'Sixpence, ninepence, a shilling on the right! One an' three, one an' sixpence on the left'. Great days. One way of making money was to look after the cars for the people who used to visit the cinema. They parked their cars on the old Market Terrace, (now of course Queensway), making sure that nobody interfered with them, I've made a few bob like that.

Another one of my pleasures was the New Theatre. I could get into the Gallery for 3d to see a first rate variety show for that! I'd sit on wooden bench seats in the Gallery, which were replaced only recently, to watch artists like Norman Evans, Sandy Powell, Kevin O'Conner, Wee Georgie Wood, Frank Randle, Hetty King, Danny La Rue and Larry Grayson in *Soldiers in Skirts*, to name a few. All great entertainers. I also remember pantomimes and circuses with the animals (horses, ponies and elephants) being stabled at the Royal Hotel, Nantwich Road, and having to be walked down Mill Street for each performance. The lions and bears were all kept backstage. Afterwards I would go to Ashworth's chip shop in Market Street for one pennyworth of chips in newspaper with plenty of salt and vinegar, lovely! You don't seem to get them like that these days.

Sunday morning was the time when the Salvation Army held a service on the Square with a full brass band. After the service they would march along Market Street into Victoria Street and back down Delaware Street to the Citadel on Market Terrace. Jack Hynes carried the flag at the front of the band; he was one of my neighbours.

This was a time of great unemployment and my father was on extended sick leave from his job as a gatekeeper at the General Offices for the LMS railway, no pay of course. When he was at work I would take him his meals at the weekend when he worked a twelve-hour shift and sometimes I would go with him on his rounds of the building. In the drawing office and the works manager's office there were a lot of models of railway engines in glass cases. These used to fascinate me. I was not allowed to touch them and would have been delighted to be the proud owner of one of them.

In Delamere Street lived one of the railway engineers, Mr Charles Darreck. In his garden he had a model railway, about a 7in gauge. Sometimes at weekends in the summer he would get the train steamed up and run it around the garden with a long seat truck. All the local children would be invited for a ride. The news spread like wildfire, and soon the place was full of kids. We all had a glass of lemonade while we were there. Mr Darreck also had an open-top sports car, an old blue and silver Bugatti. I don't know what he used for the fuel but it used to smell awful.

Across the road in Delamere Street from Mr Darreck lived Mrs Bickerstathe. She had two sons. The youngest son was called Richard; he was very interested in cine photography. In one of the rooms in their house he had a small cinema, which could seat about a dozen altogether. It was best clothes best behaviour otherwise you didn't go again.

In 1940 I was twelve. I found out that I could take a job after school, as things were pretty grim at home moneywise. We were allowed to work twenty hours a week as juveniles so I got myself a job as errand boy at J. Cummings the Chemist in Victoria Street. I worked five till seven in the evenings Monday, Tuesday, Thursday, Friday, and all day Saturday nine till six. For this I was paid 3s a week. I worked for Cummings for about fourteen months. Then I took a job at Wilding's cake shop. I worked all day Saturday and in the school holidays I sometimes went out on a Wednesday on the bread round. I was paid 4s for this, a cooked dinner and as much as I wanted to eat while I was on the premises, but I was not allowed to take anything home. We delivered in the then 'posh' area of Crewe, Willaston, Manor Avenue, Manor Way and the area around Park Drive. One lady in Manor Avenue always used to say that the bread was not well done enough for her and used to send me back to get another loaf. On many occasions I used to take the same one back and she would say, 'Now that's better why didn't you bring that one the first time?'

Christmas was a good time on that job with plenty of tips and I got double wages from the firm as a present. If I didn't go on the bread van, I used to help in the bakehouse. I really enjoyed working there. The chap in charge of the bakehouse was John Lunt. He lived in Bedford Street. A

Rolls-Royce Factory, Crewe how it used to look.

Victoria Street, Crewe, viewed from Market Street corner looking towards Hightown.

smashing man who looked after me like an uncle. I stayed with Wilding's until the summer of 1942, when I left St Mary's RC School and started to look for a full-time job.

George Ingham

The War From Empress Drive

The outbreak of war in 1939 coincided (almost) with the move to our brand new house in Empress Drive. At a cost of £499, a surveyor's fee of £1 and a solicitor's bill of £12, my Father committed himself to payments of £2 13s 6d per calendar month to the Leeds Permanent Building Society for the next twenty-five years. I can recall (I was then eight years of age) Neville Chamberlain's announcement that we were at war with Germany, someone said, 'Oh, dear!' and then life continued much as before. My father, the Works Metallurgist in the steelworks, was like so many other men in Crewe in a Reserved Occupation (Steelworks, Carriage works, Rolls-Royce), and was not called up. On three occasions, though, the war as seen through the eyes of a lad growing up in Empress Drive came excitingly – and hilariously – close.

The actual business of war – noise, discomfort, upset routine – arrived with the Blitz, though the number of bombs that actually fell on Crewe was not large. To a small boy in Empress Drive, the incendiary destruction of Hall o' Shaw Street was too far away to have much impact, as was the one that left a large crater by the side of the Cheshire Cheese. As for the one that fell on Alton Street, now that left a lasting impression. As the Anderson shelter shook, I screamed I recall, and my mother, hopelessly deaf, asked, 'What was that?'

This lack of serious bombing claimed one victim, though. Because of his position at the steelworks, Father, having seen myself and Mother into the safety of the Anderson shelter, then had to hurry off to the Steelworks Laboratory to oversee the balance of a 'melt' that could not be tapped until the all-clear was sounded. At these times, the world was filled with the noise of anti-aircraft fire, save to my mother, to whom, with her hearing-aid turned off, the sounds of conflict were as distant thunder. Father, however, had to brave the storm and, in the steel helmet with which he was supplied, make his way via Stewart Street to the Works Gate in Victoria Avenue. It was from one of these jaunts that he returned most put out, with a large dent in his steel helmet. Not a bomb had fallen on the borough, yet Father had been laid out by Collins' Grocers by a large lump of shrapnel – which, he spluttered, must have been from our own anti-aircraft guns! Outraged he may have been as the victim of friendly fire, but he refused all offers to replace that steel helmet for an undented one, and wore it at a slightly more rakish angle.

My mother's deafness provided a somewhat lighter view of the war. We were accustomed to helpless laughter at her misapprehensions:

Father: 'May, have you seen my galoshes?'

Mother: 'Not since last Wednesday – and I must say, he didn't look very well!' and so on.

Residents in the borough may perhaps remember the Sunday afternoon when a lone German bomber raced in at low level, and dropped a bomb on the Rolls-Royce works before the siren sounded. On that occasion Mother was taking a bath (regulation five-and-a-half inches) minus, naturally, her hearing-aid. Some time later, the following conversation took place:

Neighbour: 'Did you go to the shelter, Mrs Wright?'

Mother: 'Why?'

Neighbour: 'There's been an air raid!'

Mother: (After a moment's thought) 'Well! What a silly time to have an air raid!' – said in a tone that implied that Hermann Göring should mind his manners while a lady was bathing.

While England waited with bated breath in the spring of 1941 for the church bells to proclaim our invasion by a foreign foe, Father quietly got on with his Reserved Occupation. Whether he was relieved or frustrated by not being able to go to war properly like others in his age group I do not know. What I do know is that when the moment came for decisive action outside the confines of 'Reserved Occupation', he was not found wanting. Mistaken – perhaps. Gung-ho – maybe. But wanting – no! The whole hilarious episode had its roots some years before, when I was six, or maybe seven, when I thought I had found the best Christmas present ever.

Just where father got it from, I do not know to this day. I do remember finding it, and the awful kerfuffle that followed its discovery by an inquisitive child. Actually, what I was doing was looking for my Christmas present. By the time I was six or seven, my parents had begun to run out of places to hide presents supposedly delivered by Father Christmas. The top of the wardrobe was no longer inaccessible, since I was now tall enough to get there by dint of standing on a chair. Christmas had become a battle of wits, and whenever I was left unsupervised while Mother was occupied elsewhere, I was on the hunt in all sorts of nooks and crannies in the houses we occupied in Clydesdale Avenue and Empress Drive (Number Six and Number Five respectively).

When I found the flat box at the back of the drawer in Father's desk, I thought I had struck gold. This had to be it! It was damned heavy, though, as I dragged it forward over the document wallets that lay in front of it, and it was too heavy to lift out smoothly when I did get it to the edge of the drawer. Wow! I thought, as it thudded on to the carpet, some Christmas present this!

I lifted the lid with trembling hands, to reveal a cloth-wrapped object that smelled of oil. And when I unfolded the cloth from the object, I nearly fainted away! They had bought me a gun – but such a gun! No cowboy cap-gun this! This really looked and felt like the real thing – so much so that I could hardly lift it, so heavy was it. I struggled to lift it, and point it at an imaginary enemy through the window.

The piercing scream that broke my imaginative encounter with the Chinese criminals in the back-alleyways of Limehouse (last week's cinema trip), brought me as near to a heart attack as I imagine you can get at seven years of age. There in the doorway of Father's den stood my mother, having several kinds of fit. The screams ended abruptly as she fainted and was replaced in the doorway by my father, just home from work. 'It's all right, old chap, just give it to me,' he said, and then swooped to relieve me of my Christmas present. I never saw my present again until 1941.

I can recall my parents 'having words' – words like, 'Of all the incredibly stupid things to leave lying around,' which was not quite true, since it had taken some finding. The atmosphere warmed up again with the arrival of Christmas, though the Hornby Train Set was something of a letdown after that marvellous gun I thought I was going to get. Such an upset had my discovery caused that, though only a child, I was constrained to curb my curiosity and not ask questions. But why buy such a wonderful toy gun, if it were not for me? The years and events pushed the matter out of mind, if not of memory. A war broke out, and the forbidden subject was raised again, this time providing some clues regarding the strange events of the Christmastide when I was somewhat younger.

'Well,' I overheard Father say to Mother, 'I'm not handing mine in, and that's flat. They expect me to hold Hitler's paratroopers at bay while I destroy my records, but with what?' I should explain before we go any further that the Government had decreed all weapons in private hands were to be handed in to police stations, with no questions asked.

Now, I understood why Mother had thrown such a monumental wobbly. Now I understood why Father had come in for such a record-breaking ear bashing. Wartime comic papers and the illustrated adventures of their heroes had by this stage of the war

Victoria Street, Crewe looking towards Market Street.

familiarized schoolboys with items of the German armoury. Now, as the pennies fell into place, I recognized that Christmas present I had never had was not a toy at all – it was a genuine 9mm Lüger pistol, most probably of First World War vintage.

As I heard Father reiterate that he was not going to surrender it, a further penny dropped – it was no use to anyone up against an invading army unless the owner had ammunition for it. That day in 1937 or '38 when I had waved the gun around, it had been loaded! Further covert eavesdropping revealed that the gun had been hidden, minus its trigger, on top of the cold water tank in the airing cupboard since that day. The trigger, I gathered, was hidden somewhere else, and the clip of ammunition was in Father's desk, locked away.

All this was rather too much for a young lad to take in, but I was wise enough to know that Father was breaking the law in holding on to the weapon, and that it was something I could not talk about to my schoolmates. There the matter rested, while the chances of a parachute invasion dominated mealtime conversations. When, we wondered, would we hear the church bells, silenced but for this one purpose, ringing out to announce the arrival of the Herman Göring Fällscheim Jaeger in advance of the rest of the Wehrmacht?

There the matter might have rested, but for Father's bladder. Thinking the day unusually dark, even for four in the morning, he completed what he had to do, and then opened the bathroom window a crack to find silvery-grey silken material draped over the window on the outside. Not pausing to notice that there was no sound either of gunfire or of church bells, Father, in a most unscientific way, leapt to a conclusion. This was it! Not a moment to lose!

Decisive action was what was needed now so, wake the wife and the boy, and tell them to dress. Next, gather the parts of the Lüger and reassemble it preparatory to the call of duty, which meant making his way to the Laboratory, even though the boys in field-grey might try to stop him. Once there, he had simply to destroy the records of steel production, or whatever. Then, and only then, could he make his way home again to protect wife and child against the Nazi onslaught against the borough.

I can recall him coming down the stairs two at a time with the reassembled firearm in his hand. He then ushered Mother and me out of the back door into the garden and toward the Anderson shelter where, he had decided, we would be safe from the ravening Hun until he got back.

We never got there. Wallowing between our house and No. 3, with six sets of ornamental trellis hooked by its shredded cable, was a very large, partly deflated barrage balloon. Once Father was convinced that this was not a novel method of troop-delivery thought up by those awful Nazis (barrage balloons look quite different close up and soggy), I was despatched to the local RAF Balloon Barrage Station in Stewart Street (Rockwood House, as was) to alert them to the fact that one of their balloons had gone walkabout, leaving the town's

defences against the Luftwaffe seriously depleted.

Needless to say, the RAF was not at its happiest at being turned out of bed at a quarter-past four on a cold morning. Meantime, Father, all civic duty and Captain Mainwaring, had woken all the close neighbours to warn them that a barrage balloon was on the rampage. They quit their beds and went sightseeing in their dressing gowns and old macs, and then returned to their homes to make a cup of tea.

The local representatives of the RAF Balloon Barrage Command arrived (one Flight Sergeant, one Corporal and three Airmen) and had several kinds of apoplexy at the sight of smoking chimneys in the near presence of the leviathan. It was, it seemed, filled with inflammable gas, which was supposed to keep the thing airborne (but had failed this time).

When all fires had been dutifully doused, and gas stoves had ceased to boil water for tea, we stood around on that cold and tealess morn and watched the RAF fold up the balloon, and prepare to take it away. Alerted by the Air Force, a sergeant of the local constabulary arrived on his bicycle to see that the local population were not rioting or looting during this civil emergency. Throughout all these alarums and excursions Father still held the Lüger in his hand. I do honestly believe that he had completely forgotten he was holding a firearm. No one else had noticed it – at least no one was mentioning it.

The Old Bill, however, must have had sharper eyes than either our neighbours or the RAF. Sidling over to us, the attending policeman leaned across me – I can smell the tobacco on his greatcoat to this day – and said something to my father. I saw

Father look down. The policeman whispered something in my father's ear.

Father shook his head, dumbly. The policemen whispered something else, and tapped the side of his nose. The gun surreptitiously changed hands, and it disappeared forever into the capacious pocket of that tobacco-fragrant greatcoat. Thinking back, I imagine they knew each other, my father and the police sergeant; at all events, I never saw my Christmas present again.

I sometimes wonder how Father would have acquitted himself had that silvery-grey silk really been a German parachute. I like to think that he would have fought his way bravely to his laboratory and succeeded in holding off the Nazi hordes until his records were reduced to smoking ashes; and I like to think that he would have taken one or two of the enemy with him. So maybe the reality was somewhat farcical – so what? He was prepared to have a go, and that was something.

Mr W. Wright

The Second World War Through The Eyes Of A Child

When the Second World War broke out, I was four-and-a-half and lived in the West End of Crewe, quite close to Crewe Works and Rolls-Royce. I was attending the local nursery school, which was held at St Barnabas church hall, but due to the war this was closed rather prematurely.

The barrage balloons, which were put up on the field at the top of the street where I lived, Broom Street, are one of the sights I remember most vividly – perhaps these made such an impression because I was a young child. The area around us was quite rural then, lots of fields, but it has since been built up out of all recognition. The barrage balloons were huge things, hoisted quite high in the air and then anchored to the ground by steel cables. They were erected as a deterrent to low-altitude bombing because the first places the enemy aircraft looked for were Rolls-Royce and Crewe Works; both of which were situated extremely close to where I lived. The reason for this as that Rolls-Royce built the Merlin engines for all the aeroplanes and Crewe Works built steam locomotives, which were absolutely vital to our transport system. In fact, a wall which ran around part of the Crewe Works site in West Street was painted to look like a row of terraced housing so as to confuse the enemy as they flew over – quite ingenious really. It is still there today. It has faded over the years but is still worth a look. The wall runs from West Street entrance to Rolls-Royce going down as far as what was the old West Street junior school which I attended. The school has now been turned in to flats.

A huge air-raid shelter was also built on the same field, which catered for the school. Whenever the sirens went we would don our gas masks and troop across the main road from school to this shelter. We all hated our gas masks but never the less we had to put them on in case of a poisoned gas attack. This actually never happened as it turned out, but we were prepared!

I lived in a terraced block of houses and shared what was called an Anderson shelter with the people next door. These small shelters were all well and good but when it rained the whole thing would flood – you always took your wellies with you! The man next door played a banjo and he always brought it with him and we used to sit there singing songs – quite jolly really. We used to take a Primus stove to make hot drinks and took cake and biscuits. There was a lot of community spirit around in those days people really looked after each other. There was another alternative to these shelters and this was to take refuge in what was called the 'glory hole' which was actually the space underneath the stairs. Where the name 'glory hole' originated from I have no idea. But on occasions when the enemy aircraft eluded the radar and were overhead before we could get out of the house, we would often take refuge in our 'glory hole'.

I don't remember a lot of intense bombing but I do remember one night very clearly. We hadn't had time to get out to the shelter at the bottom of the garden before the bombs started dropping so we resorted to our refuge under the stairs. Quite a lot of bombs were dropped that night, although I don't remember anyone actually getting injured. Nevertheless, when day broke we couldn't get out of our house, back or front, because of the great holes the bombs had made in the ground. We had to wait until planks of wood were put into position so that we could get out – a bit like walking the plank really! But I think we were all extremely lucky that night!

Then there was the dreaded rationing! Just about everything you could think of was rationed – food, clothing, and especially petrol! People lucky enough to own a car, and there were very few in that position in those days, couldn't use them much because of the petrol rationing. The petrol that was available was needed for the war effort. Very small amounts of sugar, butter, meat, tea etc. was allocated to each person. It must have been a work of art trying to put a nourishing meal on the table in those days. We were

fortunate in some ways as my grandfather used to go out shooting rabbits and a rabbit stew could last three or four days.

There was always great excitement when the American convoys came in to town as the soldiers always had loads of chewing gum and they would throw packet after packet to the children waiting in the streets as they drove by.

There were no big supermarkets in those days. I supposed the biggest shop in Crewe then was the Co-op, which sold just about everything and there were lots of corner shops around. The big day at these shops during the war was when a fruit delivery was expected. Oranges and bananas came into the shops very rarely and there were always big queues on the day of the fruit delivery.

Another thing that happened was that all the road signs were removed so that should an invasion take place, the enemy wouldn't know where they were or where they were heading. It probably wouldn't have taken them too long to find out which part of the country they were in but it was all about delaying tactics.

Then in 1940 the Government announced that a citizens army, called the Local Defence Volunteers was being formed (later renamed the Home Guard) and men between seventeen and sixty-five who were interested in joining had to report to their local police station. The formation of the Home Guard gave those men, who for one reason or another were not eligible to be called up in the normal way, the chance of doing their bit in the defence of Britain. My father volunteered and I can remember him practising his 'present arms' routine with a yard brush. One evening he came back from an exercise looking thoroughly washed out, as well as extremely muddy. Apparently they had been crawling across a very wet and muddy field on their stomachs, holding their rifles over their heads to keep them dry. Poor Dad, he was absolutely exhausted!

When it was announced that the war was over, all the lights were switched on, shop windows were lit up again and flags flew everywhere. There were people singing and dancing in the streets. I can remember my mum and dad taking me into the centre of town to Crewe Square, and what with the lights and music and everyone dancing, it seemed like a fairytale. People were so relieved that the war was finally over.

Phyllis Greene

The Day Dunkirk Came to Crewe

It was a sunny day in June 1940, my Dad had been called up and joined the army in November 1939; my Mum had taken his place assisting my Grandfather to run the family newsagents and toy shop in Edleston Road, and I was nine years old.

Suddenly I heard a tramping of feet so I dashed out of the shop to see a group of soldiers marching, now slowly walking down the road very wearily. A sergeant shouted out 'Left, left, left – right – left' with some response from the troops.

It appeared that they had been evacuated from the beaches of Dunkirk and upon arriving back in England, placed on a troop train, travelling north to various destinations.

Upon leaving the train at Crewe the contingent were greeted by a single police constable who lead the way from the station to the Drill Hall in Myrtle Street where they were to be billeted.

As the troops progressed down Edleston Road they didn't look like British soldiers – some had equipment, others had none and their only possessions were what they stood up in, however most had rifles hung over their shoulders.

Some looked as if they hadn't washed for days, many were unshaven and most had a dazed look in their eyes.

People stood motionless and watched, some older women cried whilst small boys followed. I don't think that there were two soldiers from the same regiment – just a gathering of men who had been put on a train to Crewe.

At their arrival at the Drill Hall a senior NCO shouted the command 'Halt, right turn; right dress; fall out' – at this point some sat on the pavement whilst others ventured up the steps into the Drill Hall.

Within minute's residents of Myrtle Street appeared with jugs of hot tea, hastily prepared sandwiches and cake. The residents of lower Derrington Avenue, Lawton Street and Electricity Street quickly repeated this. The hungry but very appreciative soldiers very quickly ate the food.

Later in the day an Army vehicle arrived with a supply of palliasses which were unloaded. That night following washing and shaving, the troops settled down on the floor for their first full night's sleep after many days.

Next morning my grandfather asked me if I would like to do my bit for the war effort, Feeling very proud, I quickly set off to the Drill Hall with a newspaper bag full of morning papers to sell. *The Daily Sketch, Herald, News Chronicle* and *Daily Despatch* alas are now all gone, together with the *Daily Mirror* and of course 'Jane' the forces sweetheart. My appearance was greeted warmly and I had soon sold out, I was rewarded with a mug of army tea, the soldiers were looking more relaxed.

During that day more equipment arrived: metal bunk beds which were dispersed around the hall and cooking equipment which found a home in the existing indoor rifle range which was converted into a cook-house and mess-hall.

Each day I took my bag of papers to sell, my wages being a daily mug of tea plus a bacon butty.

On one visit I noticed the men were wearing new uniforms. Equipment had been issued and further stores and rations had been received by the acting RQMS Slowly but surely morale and confidence was returning to the men.

Within days daily orders appeared on the notice board and the NCOs started drilling the men, marching up and down Myrtle Street followed by guard duties, fatigues and inspections.

After several weeks a new battalion had been formed. I was informed by the Sergeant that they would be leaving the next morning and papers would not be required.

I went along the next morning, without my newspaper bag, to wave off the friends I had made. Tommy, Billy, Jack, Taff and many others. Slowly the neighbours who befriended them weeks earlier spilled on to the street and watched as the soldiers climbed onto the army vehicles.

One by one the vehicles roared into life as their engines were turned on. Then slowly they drove off along Myrtle Street before turning and disappearing into Edleston Road with people waving goodbye. I am sure there were a few wet eyes.

I often wondered how many of them survived the war and remembered the day when the train stopped at Crewe station and heard a loud voice shout 'All Change!'

Gerald Elson

Errand Boy In The West End

Doing errands at the local Co-op was something out of this world. I can still remember that the cashier was situated high up in the roof in a booth, which was in the far corner of the store. There were many wires going to the booth in the roof from all the different counters in the store, there was a different counter for each type of food you required e.g. butchers, hardware, dairy products, washing powder and soap. All customers had a dividend number, which you told to the counter assistant when buying goods. The dividend was paid as a one-off payment twice a year, and was used at Christmas to help with the Christmas shopping.

All the counters had a steel tube with a screw top, which was attached to the wire above there counter with a wire hanging down from it which ran to the main cashier in the roof.

The cashier put your money into it with a list and prices of all the goods you had purchased. They then pulled on the wire hanging down from their counter, and the tube seemed to glide across the top of the roof to the cashier in the booth, who looked at the list and prices, then returned it to the counter from which it had come, using the same method, with your change if any and a receipt.

Doing errands at the local Co-op for my mother and close friends and neighbours was well worth it. I was rewarded with 3d

The rear of property in Charles Street, showing the backs of houses and rear alleyway. Now the site of the British Home Stores.

The rear of property in Charles Street facing west from Wellington Street.

from one small errand, up to 6d for a big errand. Enough to pay to go to the Crewe Alexandra football match, buy a programme, a cup of tea and a pork pie, and still have money left over. I thought I was loaded at the time, but being a young boy, I did not know the meaning of money, but I was having a great time.

Faralls was situated in West Street near the top end, where there is now a petrol filling station. Faralls was a wonderland to a small boy like me, with toys, footballs, cricket bats, tennis rackets in the big shop window. There was a huge selection of pushbikes, and anything else connected with sport. On the way home from school my mates and I would go and gaze in the window dreaming of what we would have if we had plenty of money.

I used to earn another 3d from my dad if I took the wireless accumulator to be charged at Faralls. The accumulator was about half the size of a car battery today so; you can see how much power was needed to run the wireless.

The wireless is better known today as the radio, this was the only form of entertainment in those days. The wireless needed an aerial which was erected at the bottom of most peoples backyard and must have been 15ft high so it could receive the signal. We could not afford to have the wireless on all the time so my dad was very selective in using it. I can remember coming home from school at lunchtime, and my dad would switch the wireless on and we would listen to *Workers' Playtime*, which was nearly always live from a factory canteen somewhere in the country.

Workers' Playtime was a variety show, and was introduced by a celebrity of the day, the show usually contained comedians and popular singers of the time.

At night-time on the wireless we always listened to the 6 o'clock news and weather forecast. Later in the evening my mam and dad would stop everything they were doing, so that they could listen to the *Black and White Minstrel Show*, *Sing Something Simple*, and *Have a Go*. These were some of the most popular programmes of the 1950s.

Mr Ted Tunstall

CHAPTER 3

A Railway Story

Crewe Railway Works First Aid Team in the 1940s.

The Crewe Works deviation chimney (now on the road to Morrison's supermarket). This was demolished in the 1970s.

Railway Staff Drinking Alcohol on Duty?

A token purchased from a local junk shop some thirty years ago was described as a beer token once used in Crewe Locomotive Works. The acquisition turned out to be no such thing but the subject was so fascinating that it seemed to be well worth making a few enquiries.

Employees of our railways today must take special care even when drinking alcohol whilst off duty in case they happen to be over the limit when they turn in for work the following day. A positive result means instant dismissal. It is true to say that drinking whilst on duty has generally been looked upon as a very serious offence for railway workers but it

was not the case for certain employees in the Crewe Locomotive Works in the nineteenth and early twentieth centuries.

It may seem strange when looking at an old map of Crewe Locomotive Works to find it includes the Bessemer Hotel, which stood in Richard Moon Street just outside the walls of the Works. The reason for this is explained below.

On 11 October 1874 a grand fête was held in the West End of Crewe to celebrate the opening of a new public house, the Bessemer Hotel. The new hotel's licence had been transferred from the former Bessemer Vaults, which had stood in Bessemer Street, the site of which had been purchased by the London & North Western Railway Company for the erection of their new steelworks.

The new Hotel was therefore built for the Brewery Company (Greenall-Whitley) by arrangement with the London and North Western Railway. The opening ceremony was performed by the influential railway official Mr H.F. Winby. The hotel was a coach house where post horses were kept for hire. It had an excellent skittle alley where patrons could play what was then one of the working man's most popular forms of entertainment. Eventually the alley was transformed into a beautiful lawn and the old coach house into a stage for the entertainment of customers. In 1934 it was reported that the painted notice Horses for Hire 'was somewhat faded'.

The hotel was erected in that place as a facility for the nearby melting furnaces, forge and casting pits. The heat in those places was so intense that the foundry workers were allocated a free daily beer ration! In those days it was the belief that those working in such conditions should replenish lost body fluid by drinking copious draughts of ale and it was suggested that to drink water in such circumstances would be harmful to their health!

The works management issued metal

Centenary of Crewe Works in 1943. Here are employees who at that time had completed fifty years service or more.

Crewe Railway Works, Mechanical and Electrical Engineers Department at the training school in 1955.

tokens to enable these special grades of staff to claim their entitlement. Tokens were preferred to using cash in order to avoid workers forgoing their drinks and using the money for other purposes. When workmen were allowed to have a drink they would hand over their tokens to the 'beer lad' who would take the orders over to the Bessemer Hotel and return carrying the cans of foaming beer on his shoulder, suspended from a custom-made iron bar from which hung a series of hooks. The railway company would then settle up on the basis of the number of tokens collected by the landlord. The Bessemer

Hotel was unique in so much as it had a twenty-four hour licence.

So far as it can be ascertained the metal token system ceased around the time of the First World War and after that paper chits controlled settlement of accounts for the beer until the practice was discontinued.

Over the years a number of retired employees that were interviewed could remember the 'beer lads'. However, none (except that bought in the junk shop) of the metal tokens have ever turned up and the answer seems to be that they were probably crudely made in the works and

The Bessemer Hotel, Richard Moon Street.

whilst they were readily recognised by those who used them, they probably did not state on them the obvious inscription e.g. Crewe Locomotive Works Foundry One Pint. If they had it is almost a certainty that some more would have survived.

On 11 October 1974 the writer and a Crewe friend, Tom Raiswell, visited the Bessemer Hotel. There was no bunting or great celebrations as there had been when the pub had opened 100 years earlier. Only one elderly gentleman sat in a dark corner of the then dreary public house. A relief landlord sat behind the bar on a chair with his feet up, watching a television on the wall. After buying drinks, we asked him whether he was aware that the pub was 100 years old that very day. He gave a disinterested shrug of the shoulders, pushed our drinks towards us and after depositing the money in the till, resumed his viewing position without saying a word. We drank up and sadly left. The Bessemer Hotel closed its doors for the last time in August 1978 and was demolished around 1980.

Brian Edge

CHAPTER 4
Crewe People

The Vine Hotel (Nos 41-43 Earle Street).

Vernon's second beerhouse, now named Belle View Inn (No. 82 Earle Street).

The First Publican in Crewe

Even a cursory glance at the 1841 Census for Monks Coppenhall reveals no publicans or innkeepers trading in the town before the foundation of Crewe. However, such evidence offered by the census is misleading, for there had been a beerhouse on Nantwich Road before 1841. The first individual in Monks Coppenhall to take advantage of the 1830 Beerhouse Act, and a man who can, quite rightly, be called the father of the licensed trade in Crewe, was an enterprising shoemaker called John Vernon.

John Vernon was born in Minshull Vernon, three miles to the northwest of Church-Coppenhall. In July 1827 he married Elizabeth Robinson from Haslington and the couple settled in Monks Coppenhall. Vernon supported his family in the trade of 'cordwainer', or shoemaker. Vernon combined his duties as a publican with his skills as a shoemaker and offered shoemaker as his primary occupation to the Censor in 1841. He was a tenant of local landowner Richard Edleston. John Vernon's beer shop and gardens was situated on roughly the same plot of land as where the British Lion public house at No. 58 Nantwich Road is today, though there is no connection between the two businesses.

Initially, Vernon took his trade from the traffic flowing along the Nantwich to Wheelock wharf turnpike. (now Nantwich Road). This trade would have received an additional boost after the opening of Crewe station in 1837. Vernon's business venture ended when the Royal Hotel was built on Nantwich Road, in close proximity to Crewe station, towards the end of 1841. The Royal Hotel was a far superior drinking establishment than John Vernon's beerhouse, offering first class accommodation, no doubt, taking away his trade.

Vernon never completely abandoned the local licensed trade in Monks Coppenhall, for after the demise of his first business venture, he established another public house known as the Bridge Tavern at No. 6 Small Lane (the old name for Hungerford Road and much of Earle Street). Ever the astute entrepreneur, Vernon had probably noted the building of railway repair shops and workers houses in Monks Coppenhall between 1841 and 1843 and, importantly, the lack of a licensed trade in the area to service the alcoholic needs of the new arrivals. The position of the Bridge Tavern

seems to confirm this, for the building was situated just over the Liverpool Bridge from the centre of Monks Coppenhall and just yards away from the first residential district bordered by the Earle, Lyon, Forge and Sandon Streets (now the Vine Hotel).

As well as owning the Bridge Tavern, John Vernon also owned a residential property, which was built in 1816 and situated on Small Lane towards the Manchester Bridge.

In 1851, with the foreseeable ending of the depression at the Works and with the local licensed trade in Crewe promising future growth and expansion, Vernon decided to increase the number of licensed premises under his ownership and his second house on Small Lane became a beerhouse, now the Bell View Inn (No. 82 Earle Street).

John Vernon's grave in Coppenhall cemetery.

This beerhouse, situated towards the Manchester Bridge on Earle Street, derived its business not only from the growing residential district surrounding the town centre, but also from the passing trade that flowed down Hungerford Road from Sandbach and Alsager towards Crewe. Out of the two premises, Vernon chose to live at the Bell View Inn possibly because it was of a larger size, whilst he installed a tenant at the Bridge Tavern. There was also a plentiful supply of available land surrounding the Bell View Inn which, with the commercial ambition of a common brewer, Vernon utilized for the construction of a mineral water plant.

Towards the end of his life (John Vernon died on 28 August 1870, aged sixty-eight), the wine and beerhouse act of 1869 re-introduced restricted licensing in England and Wales. Amongst the many licences that were withheld in 1869, were those of the Bell View Inn and the Bridge Tavern. A man whose personal fortunes had blossomed in the period of relaxed licensing after 1830, and who had spent his entire career in an unsupervised licensed trade where the powers of justices were markedly nullified. Vernon now found that his whole livelihood was taken away from him. Asked by the justices to produce witnesses to testify to his 'good character' – one of the four criteria which were used by the justices to remove beerhouse licenses, Vernon took the unprecedented step of bringing no one into the courtroom, but himself. A ruse which, thirty years on would have been considered contemptuous and deserving of instant license removal. The Nantwich justices were somewhat amused by the attitude of this old man, after he had explained that he was the longest serving publican in Crewe. The police gave the justices the necessary 'good character' reference. The license of the Bell View Inn was then renewed.

After the death of John Vernon, Elizabeth Vernon took control of the two public houses and of the mineral water business. One of her first acts of ownership was to change the name of the Bridge Tavern to 'The Vine Inn'. After Elizabeth Vernon's death, the business was passed on to her son, William John Vernon.

Nigel Ansell-Roberts

A Popular Crewe Man

The popular Crewe character, Levy John Joyce, was born around 1856 in Sherington near Newport Pagnell in Buckinghamshire, and as a young man moved to Crewe to work as a railway engine fitter.

A photograph depicting a terraced house with a man standing on the doorstep inspired this piece of research. The photograph would have been meaningless had not someone crudely scribbled in pencil on its face 'Mr Joyce at Door...Samuel Street'.

Levy John Joyce named his residence at No. 11 Samuel Street Crewe 'Sherington House' after his birthplace.

He was promoted to Chief Foreman in No. 9 Erecting Shop in 1888 and had charge of 700 mechanics. He was responsible for all the new engines manufactured in the Works between his appointment and his untimely death on 26 February 1910.

Mr Joyce was connected with many public service movements and he rendered good service to the town. He showed

Number 11 Samuel Street, Crewe, Levy John Joyce at the door.

familiar figure driving his horse and trap around Crewe and district. The stable where he kept his horse is still at the rear of No. 11 Samuel Street.

Joyce died at the young age of fifty-four after a short illness. The Works Manager, A.R. Trevithic wrote to him during his illness and an extract from Joyce's reply read:

'I am very sorry that I have had to give up again so soon but I will take your advice and not come in again until I have thoroughly recovered. You have been kind to me on many occasions and I am truly grateful.'

Three days later, Joyce succumbed to influenza. The Chief Mechanical Engineer C.J. Bowen-Cooke personally wrote a letter of condolence to the widow and in her reply she wrote:

abounding enthusiasm in the work of the Cottage Hospital where he was a Life Governor. He was also interested in the Euston Coffee Tavern where he assisted in keeping it in working order and subsequently raising valuable funds for the Cottage Hospital. Joyce was also an active member of the Fête Committee and he acted, on occasions, as a judge, where he exhibited care, patience and impartiality in making awards. He was for thirty-two years a member of the Grand United Order of Oddfellows and Secretary of the Loyal Perseverance Lodge of that movement. He was passionately fond of horses and was a

The house name plaque, above Mr Joyce's door at No. 11 Samuel Street Crewe, named after his place of birth.

'The fact that your letter was written by your own hand makes it all the more valued as an indication of your personal sympathy. The letter will always remain one of our treasured possessions...I feel sure you will pardon me if I say, that the Railway Company never had a more loyal servant than he was; and it would have been a great joy to him could he but have known of your appreciation of his services.'

Levy John Joyce was buried, with a headstone, in Crewe Cemetery. His life typifies thousands of men who over the years were equally loyal to their employers in Crewe Works and who contributed in their own way to the success of the town.

The contributor would like to thank Harry Jones, Mrs Edna Redwood, Howard Crawford, Mr Jack Sylvester and Mrs Mary Hamlin for their assistance with this piece.

Brian Edge

In Search of Harry Piggott

Gran Davies brought the book out every year, just as the cold bit the few inches between my grey flannel shorts and woollen stocking tops. She carefully unwrapped it from between brown paper sheets and thin tissue, laying every piece alongside the book with great care, as if the whole thing had to be executed according to ritual. The rules were embedded, no doubt, from her years as custodian of these pages. It wasn't unlike the big Holy Bible Miss Tunstall gave Granddad before she died, with a list of names written in the back in a neat hand, weaving black ink into births, marriages and deaths. These pages were covered in names too, but in lists, neatly stacked one upon the other, in printed and precise regiments. The rest of the ritual was quiet and included tears, none spilling on the pages, on the names. She caught her sadness in a handkerchief, wrapped it back into her apron pocket then folded the sheets around the book and took it upstairs to where it was enshrined in the dark wardrobe, next to Granddad's bowler hat, and the carved stick from India.

And eventually I grew up and forgot about it, and she died, and the book disappeared.

Some years later Auntie Edna said I could poke through the stuff she'd got upstairs in the trunk under the bed. I was eager to get there, root around the stuff she called rubbish because Uncle Doug, before he died, had been a great Crewe Alexandra fan, and maybe there would be a pile of programmes, maybe even Tottenham Hotspur *versus* Crewe Alexandra, 13-2. There wasn't. Cousin Graham was pictured at a few months, a few years, another few years, in school uniform, in knitted jumpers, with and without glasses, swimming, playing football, playing the fool, but then, under his history, I found the brown paper, and the tissue, and the book.

'Uncle Harry's book,' Auntie Edna said, 'Mam's brother. Harold John Piggott. You can borrow it if you like.'

I didn't have to invent a ritual. I already knew one. No words came to mind, no instruction on how to look, what to look for. The cover, in gold block stated,

ROLL OF HONOUR
LONDON AND NORTH WESTERN RAILWAYMEN
WHO LOST THEIR LIVES WHILE SERVING
WITH HIS MAJESTY'S FORCES DURING THE
GREAT WAR 1914-1918

Inside, in the regiments of loss I found, 'Piggott H.J. Cleaner (Loco), Stafford, Driver. My history of World War One began.

Auntie Edna unpacked memories of Uncle Harryn and showed me a photograph of her standing on the window ledge at No. 6 Clark Street, Crewe, where he lived with Jane Ellen Piggott, his mother, and his sister Nellie, my Grandmother who unpacked her loss each November during my childhood.

Through the Internet I discovered the Commonwealth War Graves Commission website, and after typing in the few details I knew, read down the list of Piggotts who had died during the war. Harold John, of No. 6 Clark Street, Crewe, was listed. He died on 5 November 1914, aged eighteen. A young man. It named his next of kin, Jane Ellen, and specified the plaque number on the Menin Gate, Ypres, which commemorates his death, and brief existence. If he was buried there were no records of where.

I wanted to know more, wanted to see something more of him, how he looked and lived, and if anyone of us looked like him. Most of all I wanted to make sense of how a young man died like this, and how I could thank him, keep his memory alive. I'd found that his existence was merely a record, a name, a number, and a date. He had to be more than this.

I'd not used microfiche before. The librarian loaded the film, showed me how to turn and wind the machine, and how to magnify the pages. The *Crewe Guardian* for the year 1914 revealed a strange history. Alongside the notices for a Whist Drive, and local Flower and Vegetable Show, a list of names grew week by week. Deaths. Casualties. Missing. Sometimes a report indicated more explicitly how someone had died, but even that felt remote, almost

fictional. The year 1914 revealed nothing of Harry. Nothing on a list. No article.

A few weeks later the same librarian sighed as she loaded another film – *Crewe Chronicle*, 1914. I asked for 1915 too, just in case. I sat down, fumbled with my glasses, and as soon as I was able to focus on the page, I saw it:

A Soldier's Mother in Trouble.

'At Crewe Police Court on Saturday, Ellen Piggott of Clark-street was charged with having been drunk and disorderly in Clark-street on the previous evening. Supt Thompson said there were a number of previous convictions against the accused. She had a son in the army and was allowed 3s a week whilst he was away. If she continued her conduct she was liable to lose this amount. The accused has promised to mend her ways and was fined 2s 6d and costs.'
Crewe Chronicle, Saturday, 26 December 1914.

It was his mother! My great-grandmother! 'A number of previous convictions'? I wanted to laugh, until it struck me that by this time her son had been killed! She couldn't have known – the article indicated that he was still alive. I rolled the film back to November, and worked carefully through the pages. Nothing. The film flipped out of its case as I came to the end. I loaded 1915, and again, with careful scrutiny scanned each column, each list, every name. I found it. A tiny fragment beneath a list of casualties:

Another Crewe Soldier Killed

'Information received this week to the effect that Driver H.J. Piggott of the ASC whose mother recently resided in Clark-street,

Crewe, had been burnt to death in France. It is supposed that he was out with a motor car, which caught fire, and he received fatal burns.'

Crewe Chronicle, Saturday, 20 February 1915.

So this is history? To find out the tragedy of two lives lived and lost. A mother's alcoholism, a son's premature death? My feelings were a confusion of sadness and anger. I'd grown up in a generation that hadn't experienced war directly, and I had a tinted vision of mothers crying as their sons marched heroically to their deaths. I weep for him now. I weep for Jane Ellen too. She'd been through the humiliation of the court without the knowledge that her son had been killed. If it created a riot of questions for me now how would people have been with her then? Crewe was a small town, and the scandal would have run for a time no doubt, only to be refreshed by Harry's death. 'The woman who drank while her son burned to death in Ypres.'

I thought of Nellie Piggott's history, my Gran Davies. She would have lost her brother, suffered her mother's drinking, been in service at the age of fourteen, married by eighteen, and widowed by nineteen when the influenza epidemic took her husband away. No wonder the intensity of her annual ritual of the book and remembrance. If only I'd known then, as a child, I'd have asked her more, consumed every word so that lives would be more than details on a plaque, or paragraphs in a newspaper. Maybe now I'd make some sense of this. How did she live with it? How exactly did he die? Why did she drink?

History won't furnish me with details of Jane Ellen's agony of loss and shame, or gentle down the images of how Harry died,

but last November (2000), standing on Crewe Town Square, just before the Remembrance Day Service, I read the plaques under the War Memorial and found his name. I realized standing there on that spot, I stood where Jane Ellen must have done, her head bowed, tears spotting the bronze tablet as mine did. My tears were for both of them, for their frailty, for lives I barely understand and can't forget.

I repacked the book with care. Auntie Edna says that when she dies she'll donate it to a Railway Museum. I look at the scanned images of the pages commemorating Harry's death, faded and hard to read, hard to understand. Like history.

Michael A. Robinson

The Oakley Street Invasion

My mother was a well-known and respected woman in Crewe: Ethel Brown, mother of her own ten children and surrogate mother to half the kids in Oakley Street. She knew everybody and everybody knew her.

To go shopping with her was like a Royal walkabout. People would stop her on every corner. She would listen and give good advice to troubled souls. She was outspoken and down to earth, so sometimes the advice didn't please some people, but that was my mother. Take it or leave it!

She had great community spirit, where there was a party to be held in the street she would take charge. Dad was sent to the Lesser Hall in Co-Operative Street to hire trestles, benches and giant tea urns.

Mrs Brown, as everyone respectfully called her, was the organizer of 'The Grand Trip to the Seaside', of which she organized many. This was the late 1930s or early '40s and very few had their own transport, although our headmistress at Beech Street School had an Austin Seven. A few in the street had bikes.

The venues for these coach trips were always decided on the journey home from the one before. People would wing ideas down the coach, 'What about Llandudno next Mrs Brown?'. She would have a show of hands to decide. The very next pay-day the collections would start, I held the money bag and notebook and one shilling or half a crown was collected from each participating household every week until the next outing was due. By then the coach fare was paid and all children would get pocket money back to spend.

Friday night was collection night and I loved it. I felt quite important as I entered

One of Ethel Brown's day trips ready for a coach ride to the seaside.

the payments in my notebook. Most of the children went free as long as they sat on the parent's knee, if a child were older Mam would say, 'Have you got a stool to put in the gang way?'.

Most coaches held around thirty-six people but never less than seventy got on! Sometimes the demand was so great that two coaches were booked. I don't ever remember the driver complaining about overloading. He always used to get a good whipround on the way home and was fed all day by the mothers.

For our first trips, Mam always booked a Crosville coach, until one day the coach they sent us had wooden seats and was well past its best. Mam refused to accept it. She reared up to her full height of 5ft and with arms folded said, 'We are not cattle, young man. Take it back and bring a proper coach. Tell your boss Mrs Brown insists'. Formidable woman, my mother! He returned shortly with the newest coach they had. There were cheers from the waiting day-trippers.

We went everywhere within an eighty-mile radius. Blackpool was always a popular venue, at least once a year. When the illuminations began again after the war it was magical. Us kids had never seen anything like it; there were glowing, wide-eyed faces at every window of the coach.

We would invade Corr's fish and chip shop on arrival and eat out of the paper as we strolled along the prom twenty abreast.

At Llandudno we would take over the Great Orme and Happy Valley. The mountain railway to the top of the Orme was buzzing on our days.

Went to Southport but couldn't find the sea!

We visited Morecombe but it was closed, so we never went back.

A trip to a stately home: quite a fiasco that was, Lord and Lady so and so, wondered what had happened when our coach arrived. It was the poor peacocks on the lawn that I felt sorry for, don't think they had been lasso'd before!

My mother organized these trips for a good twenty-five years. Most people who lived around us would never have gone anywhere in the early days without these trips and would probably never have seen the sea! She gave a lot of hard-up families a chance of a break from their hand-to-mouth existence.

We moved away from the town centre in the late 1940s and went to live in the West End of Crewe. Mother went on to organize more trips in our new neighbourhood to the delight of the residents there.

The days out dwindled towards the late 1950s as people began to get their own transport as our family did. Mrs Brown is still remembered by the kids in our streets, most of whom are parents and grandparents themselves now.

Sadly missed by her family and all that knew her, Mrs Brown was one of Crewe's true characters.

Joan Bebbington (née Brown)
Prize Winner

Ash Wednesday, 1988

It is the stuff of every schoolchild's favourite daydream. The school is burnt down, right to the ground. Well, it happened to our school on Ash Wednesday, 1988. The fire brigade was called out to a dustbin fire in the early hours of the morning, only to find that Gainsborough County Junior School was burning out of control. A few hours later it was nothing but a charred, burnt-out shell. We had no school to return to after the half-term holidays.

I am not sure how we found out what had happened – I think the news just spread, like a good old-fashioned rumour. I remember eavesdropping on my mother's telephone conversation trying to guess what had happened. There was no need to guess really, she told me straight afterwards. It seemed the kind of thing that happened to other people, certainly not the sort of thing that happened in Crewe, where nothing of merit appeared to have happened since the advent of the railways a century and a half earlier. I was gripped by a sort of awed excitement, more at the thought of being at the centre of a real live event than at the joy of having no school to go to. We stayed up to watch the news and see our moment of fame. We had to wait ages, but at last I was satisfied that Crewe was on the national map, complete with a dramatic picture. In reality, I suppose the reason for the long wait was that our story was actually on *NorthWest Tonight*, not the national news at all, but to my nine-year-old self, the whole world knew about us.

It wasn't that I hated school. In fact, I loved my school, I liked the way its classrooms were arranged like steps running from the first year to the fourth year. I liked my lessons. I liked writing and painting and playing with my friends (but not maths and PE). I also liked my third year teacher – Miss Hatton. We were afraid of her at first and there were rumours that she was very strict. She was, but very nice nevertheless. She let us sew instead of going to choir and she entertained us with stories about her little dog Pip. Most of all, though, I liked our headmaster, Mr Jennison, with his funny assemblies, his love of creative writing classes, where he repeatedly told us that only boring poetry rhymed, and his habit of assigning everyone little nicknames, of which no one quite knew the origin (often including him).

On the other hand, I was nine years old and there is nothing more exciting than a drama or a crisis, particularly one which makes a good story and provokes jealousy in other children.

We had, of course, been warned endlessly about the dangers of fire. We could recite backwards the familiar mantras: 'Leave the building immediately; do not stop to collect possessions; walk, don't run; assemble on the playground; do not under any circumstances at all, return to the scene of the fire'. In the event, and rather disappointingly, we did not get the chance to put any of this into practice, as the school burned down at night, in the school holidays, set alight by arsonists. Even so, there was no shortage of drama, some of it more immediate and frightening than I had expected.

My mum took us to look at the site the next day. I was amazed by how much it had become a 'site'. It was no longer my school. It looked like a giant had taken a large and messy bite out of it. There was still a faint smell of smoke and everything looked very black, I remember seeing things like chairs and asking my mum if they could be saved. She said not, as there was too much smoke damage and the things would stink. She said it was a miracle that they had salvaged the school record books, though they were somewhat charred.

Back at home, it was a week of rumours. The most exciting one was that of an extra weeks holiday. We were asked to make lists of anything important we thought we might have lost in the fire. All I could think of was my recorder, lying in my little plastic locker. My mum said it would be a melted heap by now, and anyway it wasn't worth much and I never practised it. I think that both she and Mr Jennison were secretly pleased at the demise of so many recorders. Mr Jennison disliked them immensely and said they were nasty squeaky things.

Unfortunately my mother pointed out that I had carelessly lost the Australian Project she had done when she was a little girl, as I had taken it in to show the class for our own project on Australia. Not only this, but I had lost a jar of shells and coral which my uncle had brought back from the Great

Barrier Reef (my uncle was very important in the navy). He still has no idea how those shells met their fate.

No one seemed to know quite what was going to happen and things seemed to become much more serious. The main question of concern to me was what would happen to 200 children with no school to go to were worried that we would be split up and distributed among other schools in the borough, none of which sounded too appealing. We were petrified of being sent to Brierley Street. I had no idea where Brierley Street was, but I knew I didn't want to go there. According to my mum's friend Gill,

Gainsborough Junior School demolished after the fire.

The fire works its way along the General Office building.

the headmaster of Brierley Street had said he wished it were his school which had burnt down. They told me he had meant it as a joke and I must, under no circumstances, repeat it.

Eventually, towards the end of the extended holiday, it was announced that King's Grove School had agreed to accommodate us. I was pleased that we would not be separated and forced among strange children, but King's Grove seemed scarier than the prospect of Brierley Street, wherever it was. The pupils at King's Grove were bigger and, as they say in Crewe, 'dead 'ard'. Still, we had no right to complain. We were allocated four classrooms inside the building for the third and forth years and the first and second years were to have mobile classrooms on the edge of the school field.

It was frightening going back to school, especially this school. It was huge compared to Gainsborough and seemed old and dusty, like *Grange Hill*. I was frightened I would get lost, or worse, meet the older pupils. The room my class was allocated seemed very old fashioned and horribly far removed from the junior school. The tables and chairs were old and wooden and covered with graffiti and discarded chewing gum of their former occupants. It seemed too grown-up.

Suddenly, school changed a lot. We were like campers or refugees and not like a community school at all. There were no more assemblies because there was no school hall. We rarely saw the other classes at all. We still had PE but it became less regular, as we had to wait till the hall was free. It also became less orthodox due to lack of equipment, and we played soft ball (whatever that was) a lot. Also, Miss Hatton had lost her class records so the first lessons we had at King's Grove were very much a case of trial and error as we tried to remember where we were up to in maths and English. There was often a great sense of déjà-vu. Our lunchtime playtimes were spent in the courtyard of the school, which was pleasant but hardly big enough for any charging around. In the afternoon, we could use King's Grove playground, but it took such a long time to walk there around the outside of the school that it was time to come back before we got there. I still enjoyed school, but it didn't seem at all like my picture of what school was and should be.

Meanwhile, we watched in wonder as the new school began to take shape. It was not in the same place as the old one, which had, according to rumour, been found to overlie the drains of South Cheshire College, meaning that should there have been a problem, it would probably have met its fate, anyway. We were encouraged to take an interest, even though we wouldn't be able to experience the finished product, as we would have to move to secondary school by then. We drew plans of how we would like the school to be, complete with robots and all the supposed trappings of the magical twenty-first century, reverently referred to as the Year 2000. We were taken to see the site and Mr Jennison encouraged us to write creatively about the JCBs and other goings on, which somehow we managed. Mrs Crocker, who did pottery, came in and helped every child in the school to make a tile for the new entrance hall. They all had something to do with the school and we etched our names in the bottom corners. Mine showed a gleaming white sink and taps. I was very proud of it.

Finally, a boy in my year designed a new logo for the school, which we were told would be emblazoned on new school sweatshirts. This was novel, as we had never had a logo before, nor had we had school sweatshirts, as Mr Jennison disapproved of uniforms, saying he didn't want us all to look the same. As for the logo, what else but the phoenix rising from the flames!

Rhonwen Saunders

Battling With Fire

It was the evening of Saturday 23 July 1983. Suddenly the loud, screaming sound of the warblers alerted each fireman on duty, sending our heartbeats into top gear, as we raced towards the fire engine from all directions, without any hesitation.

Three of us mounted the fire engine and the officer in charge followed, reading the message on the turnout sheet of paper. He then shouted, 'It's a fire at Eaton Street. The Old Railway Building.'

The big blue metal doors opened with a loud clattering noise and then I started the fire engine. I didn't have to ask which was the quickest way to go because I could see a huge dark cloud of smoke over the town centre, disturbing the natural beauty of the sky's blue and red colours.

My body was full of excitement, and my face didn't know whether to look anxious or break into a chuckle. I had waited for this moment to arrive ever since I had the desire to be a fireman, because this was my first time driving a fire engine to any kind of incident.

The strict militaristic training to become a fireman, followed by a driving course that demanded concentration far beyond my expectations was about to be put to the test. Fireman Alec Thomasson and Bob Hughes who sat behind me were busy dressing into their fire gear and discussing tactics for fighting the fire with the officer in charge Richard Green. He was shouting his orders, whilst competing with the booming racket of the two-tone horns. With these noises and the radio blaring away in my ears it was no wonder I found myself getting an adrenaline rush.

'It's going to be an all night job this one,' said one of my colleagues.

As we approached the vicinity of the smoke, hoards of people had gathered and were pointing their fingers towards the blaze. We suddenly realized the extent of the lively fire and assistance was requested with great urgency. The officer in charge held the radio handset close to his mouth and sent a piority message to the brigade control in a precise and clear manner, 'From Sub-Officer Green at British Rail General Offices, Eaton Street, Crewe, make pumps five'.

Many onlookers watched a piece of Crewe's heritage go up in flames.

Firefighters hosing down the flames from the hydraulic platforms.

The devastated building the morning after.

Before the fire: Crewe Railway General Offices.

His forehead was frowning as he anxiously assessed the risk to surrounding properties, whilst waiting for a reply to his request, for another four pumping fire engines to attend.

My first drive to a fire had suddenly come to an abrupt end, as I pulled up near the Royal Naval Association Club in Eaton Street. Orange glowing flames were licking out of the windows of the former British Rail site. The blaze was building up rapidly, with plenty of dry wood as the main source of fuel, in this historic brick property. The crackling sound of burning wood and the smell of burning embers was filling the still warm air.

Our other two colleagues, Keith Stubbs and John Spicer, arrived in the Emergency Tender, which became the incident control unit. They both scrambled to locate a vital water supply, looking like bees hunting for pollen. After a thorough search of the surrounding area it was a huge relief to see them find a convenient hydrant not too far away.

Access to the fire was gained by trampling down a bank in a small woodland, with overgrown bushes and flourishing green trees, alongside the Naval Club. Hosepipes were laid in readiness for the attack on the blaze. As I watched my colleagues, they looked like knights in yellow and black armour charging at the enemy; which was throwing out intense heat and rapidly becoming wildly out of control. As the fire gathered momentum it was spreading fiercely into the long pitched roof.

The arrival of the second fire engine from Crewe was a welcome sight. Their immediate task was to protect the threatened old railway cottages in Tollitt Street, Betley Street and Dorfold Street. These houses were in grave danger as the radiated heat started twisting and sagging their plastic guttering. The desperate occupants wasted no time evacuating their dwellings for their own safety.

The fire, engulfing anything within its grasp, was initially tackled from the outside with several water jets. Despite throwing gallons of water at the stubborn flames, they kept re-emerging, not wanting to lie down. Several more fire engines and senior fire officers had now arrived and attempts were made to try a dangerous interior attack of the fire. However, the County Deputy Chief Fire Officer who had by now taken overall command, ordered the men to withdraw all fire-fighting from inside the building, as the brutal flames looked like getting the better of the firemen inside.

'For God's sake, get those men out of there. It's a bloody death trap and I'm not taking any chances. It's only a derelict after all!' he ordered, with total command in his sharp voice.

As daylight gradually vanished, and the dark sky took over, the orange glow above the town centre became a spectacular sight with flames leaping through the burning roof. It could be seen from miles around. The attraction of the blaze was very evident, as hundreds of onlookers had now gathered to witness the destruction of a piece of Crewe's heritage.

Virtually the whole building, approximately 550ft long by 50ft wide, was engulfed in flames. Hose lines lay on both sides of the building and along Chester Bridge looking like bundles of spaghetti. Leaks of water spraying from tiny pinholes in some of the hoses provided the occasional refreshing sensation, as the fine fountain of cold water hit our perspiring faces on the fire ground, where trains once passed. Fire engines were parked everywhere; fifteen was the final count. Two hydraulic platforms, the emergency tender, a fleet of fire officers' cars, ambulances and police cars were at the hectic scene. Seven long, exhausting hours after the alarm was raised, the fire was finally under control.

The smouldering remains of timber having given way; the twisted and tangled metal beams steaming off and piled in heaps; the hot backing bricks; and the sight of about 100 weary firemen were a sign that the fire had been victorious. However the self-satisfaction shown by the firemen as they leaned on each other and shared their own personal experiences with one another was an indication that they felt triumphant.

The usual investigation to determine the cause was virtually an impossible task for the experts in this field. Arson, a very serious crime, is usually caused by someone seeking revenge or by someone seeking to make a profit. But on this occasion, after days of sifting through the rubble looking for any vital clues, the cause was assumed to be by children playing with matches.

The destruction of this building by the primitive force of fire was the final chapter in its glorious history, as part of Crewe's railway heritage disappeared overnight. With the shell of the building barely standing up, it had to be demolished on safety grounds. These former offices, constructed in 1876 had been vacant for about three years. The unique building had its front curved to align with the old Chester Rail Line and several historical events had been held here. With so many notable people from all over the world having visited the site it was due to be made into a listed building at any time.

Gareth Roberts

Tudor Times in Crewe

My father was brought up in Monks Coppenhall this being the origin of Crewe. In 1914-18 he served in the Kings Company Grenadier Guards in France in the Great War. He was later employed as a passenger guard on the railways. My mother's family came from Much Wenlock, Shropshire. Her family moved to the area when her father came to seek employment on the railways, when Crewe became the leading player in Locomotive build and repair work. My mother and father were married in Haslington, and moved in with her sister and husband in Gresty Road opposite the former railway hostel, where railway staff used to stay overnight prior to taking the train back to London. This was where I was born in 1927.

Later that year my parents were given the key to No. 26 Darlington Avenue, Crewe, a house on a large housing estate in the West End of Crewe. The avenues on this estate were named after illustrious men who, it is said, made Crewe: McNiel; Frank Webb; Kettell; Bowen Cooke and Darlington.

I was the eldest of five children. My first childhood memory was at the age of three, seeing the ill-fated R101 airship pass over

Jeff Tudor with his mother.

Crewe. My first school was at Webbs Orphanage, which had been brought into use owing to the high birth rate on the estate. I went on to attend West Street Junior School and Ludford Street Senior School where, I remember, discipline was usually a duster hitting you on the back of the head!

Saint Barnabas' church had a big impact on our lives; I attended Sunday School and was in the choir with my brother John. St Barnabas also had church lads' brigade, which was first class. Our leaders were Mr Bull and Mr Wright.

I remember Mr Wright announcing that we were at war with Germany on 3

Jeff Tudor working in the Tube Shop at Crewe Railway works in 1951.

September 1939. We all sang *God Save the King!*

During a Thursday evening choir practice, German bombers appeared over Crewe at a height of around 400ft. They dropped incendiary bombs. The foundations of the church shook, I thought the church walls were going to collapse. On this Sunday afternoon a lone German bomber had sneaked under low cloud cover and released a stick of high explosive bombs. It had taken the lives of seventeen Rolls-Royce workers. The balloon barrage defence was caught napping. Crewe suffered damage during the war due to the fact that the Merlin engines were built at Rolls-Royce and the Railway workshops were always prime targets.

We had a first class Home Guard company too. I remember Mr Barker our local warden coming to our house to give us seven gas masks. Thank God we did not have to use them. While sitting in an air-raid shelter, I remember, I told my sister I had seen a mouse – it gave her such a fright! Then it came to light that my brother had been feeding it with cheese.

Alan Cobham's flying circus and Pat Collins' fair would occasionally visit the fields on Sunnybank Road. They did a lot for the hospital charity, but this all stopped when one of the fair workers was refused treatment, after that they never came back. The fields eventually became the Rolls-Royce factory in 1938.

I was lucky enough to be accepted for an apprenticeship in Crewe Railway works

Crewe Locomotive Railway Works Tube Shop in 1952.

when I was fourteen. It was like going into Dante's *Inferno*, with the noise of the belt driven machines. I worked a forty-two-hour week. There was the usual teasing – being sent for buckets of steam and left-handed spanners. I was employed in Crewe Railway works for forty-two years and became one of the 3,000 made redundant in 1985 when a private company bought the works.

Entertainment in Crewe was provided by picture houses like The Odeon, Grand, Kino, Empire, Palace and The Lyceum theatre, not to mention the Town Hall dances, held by Mr Rattigan.

In the 1940s many public houses had sports teams, including athletics, bowling, cricket and football. The mecca of Crewe for sport was the LMS sports ground in Earle Street. I can remember a gate of 12,000 at the ground for the visit of Reg Harris and the Manchester wheelers. Crewe Wheelers had local heroes like Sprinter Jolly and Albert Crimes. Crewe Alexandra Athletic Club was formed on 20 June 1899 and many sporting events were held at the ground. Sadly to say, in 1992 there was a compulsory purchase of British Rail land. This saw the end of Crewe Sports as I knew it.

After retiring I became a member of the British Railways Institute in Prince Albert Street where our fathers had gone before us. I became a committee member and Games Secretary. Bowen Cooke and the North Western Railway Company gave the building to the town's railwaymen, to use in their twilight years. But alas another part of Crewe's heritage is under threat, for in July 2000 the building was sold for £128,000.

J.J. Tudor

Parton Bros. Travelling Shop

Harry Parton (born 1875) and his two sons, Harry (Archie) and Lawrence, provided a travelling shop service to all areas of Crewe using a horse and cart.

Harry Parton's first wife died in 1917; he remarried and had three more children Doug, Joan and Roy. In the early 1920s Lawrence immigrated to Canada.

Harry and his son Archie went out every day, as each had a horse and cart.

The travelling shops serviced all areas of Crewe, with most areas (rounds) being visited twice a week. Due to council byelaws nothing could be sold after 1 p.m. on a Wednesday under threat of a fine. Both carts carried a metal tank to hold paraffin oil; each tank held about 50 gallons. Paraffin at that time was mainly used for lighting, being sold in pints, quarts, half-gallons or gallons. Some paraffin stoves and heaters were available at that time in the 1920s and '30s but if people had no gas or electric they would cook over the coal fire. In addition to paraffin, the travelling shops carried: soap powders; buckets; dolly blues; zebo grate polish; donkey stones (for steps) and as a sign on Harry's cart proudly proclaimed, 'Glasses for all lamps'.

In fact they attempted to supply the hardware requirements of everyday living while themselves working on a tight budget.

On some rounds more paraffin could be sold than could be carried on the cart, so to avoid having to return to West Street to fill up, Mr Parton had an informal arrangement with Mr Gamwell of Walthall street who was a ShellMex tanker driver. In his Albion tanker he would meet Mr Parton at prearranged places and replenish the tank on the cart.

Crewe Works Army Cadets on Rhyl front. From left to right: Cyril Hobson, Jeff Tudor, Roy Broadfield, Derek Baker, and Roy Brereton.

During an air raid in the 1940s a garage near the stables was hit by an incendiary bomb intended for Rolls-Royce. There was a fire so Bob (the horse's name) was brought round to the backyard of the shop for the night.

When Bob came to the foot of a steep hill such as at Church Minshull or Joey the Swan he would stop and just stand nodding his head, not wanting to climb the hill. Roy remembers that the only way to get Bob to climb the hill was to 'scratch the horse's arse with a nail'!

While Doug was away in the RAF and Roy was away in the Army Harry Parton became ill. Joan took over the rounds, she did not know all the calls but the horse was so familiar with the rounds that it knew where to go and where to stop.

Sadly Harry Parton died from bowel cancer on 6 June 1944.

Harry Parton Jnr's cart.

Harry Parton with Bob the horse that would only climb a hill if you scratched his arse with a nail!

Partons Travelling Shops.

A New Era

Moving with the times Doug, Joan and Roy purchased a Morris Isis ex-ARP ambulance. This was painted and signwritten in the soon to become familiar green livery of Parton Brothers. The sign writing on the high front of van read 'Shop the easy way- Let us come to you'.

Doug was looking after the West Street shop then but when his daughter Joyce came to work in the shop Doug took over the van rounds.

A smaller Austin 30cwt van was purchased and painted in the same livery. Doug drove this van and later it was driven by Hazel Parton, Roy's wife, until Dougie Parton, Doug's son, was old enough to drive. Sadly Dougie was tragically taken from us in 1960 at the tender age of nineteen years after losing his battle with leukaemia. This van was later used for paraffin deliveries – one of a number of smaller vans acquired for this purpose over the years. These were painted in a different Pink Paraffin livery.

Roy Parton replaced his ex-Hunts van with a purpose-built travelling shop. In the 1960s with paraffin sales booming, due to the popularity of Aladdin and Valor paraffin heaters, the tanks on the vans were proving to be too small, so to avoid running back to West Street a bulk tanker was bought. Driven by Joan's husband Frank the tanker would bring paraffin out to the travelling shops very much like the arrangement Harry Parton had with Mr Gamwell years ago.

In 1963 a new Austin chassis was purchased and a purpose-built body was coach-built by Hudson's of Hanley. Roy used this travelling shop until it was taken off the road in 1981.

From the late 1970s Doug concentrated on developing the West Street shop so Roy had the sole Parton Bros. travelling shop. Generations of children will remember buying penny Arrowbars and Caramac or queuing up with a paraffin can.

During all of this period Harry Partons home, No. 135 West Street, was a hardware shop and has now evolved into a row of shops but that, as they say, is another story.

Ken Parton

Changing Crewe

For me Crewe is all about change, and I don't mean just at the railway station.

I am in my early forties, and I'm talking of a time when I was a kid around the mid-1960s, to me its not that long ago!

Mum was brought up in Station Street, now long gone. It consisted mainly of back to back terraced houses and as the name suggests, it was in the Nantwich Road part of town close to the railway station. When mum and dad married they moved to Roebuck Street, just off Broad Street, and as kids this was our area of town. You never really strayed too far from your own area and I suspect it would have been the same in mum's day.

As a kid, I remember being taken regularly, along with my sister and little brother, still in his pushchair, by Mum on a Sunday afternoon for a walk around 'The Old Park'. I could never understand why it was called this, there were no swings, slides or ice cream vans, just boring fields, nettles and blackberries.

For those of you not familiar, I'm talking of a route which took you from the station, along Weston Lane and past the entrance to Crewe Hall. From here you turned left in front of Smithy Cottage and followed the Alsager road stopping for a picnic at what we called Bluebell Wood on the right. This was really part of the Duchy of Lancaster land and I was always worried that 'she' might catch us.

Carrying on to what Mum called the Alsager turning, via Slaughter Hill, stopping to pick blackberries (try it now with all the traffic), we would carry on to Crewe Green church and back home through town.

Now, as I remember at that time, Weston Lane apart from Rollermakers on the right, Chester Barrie and I think Air Products on the left, there were open fields towards Crewe Hall woods.

Mum, on the other hand, without fail, would always tell us as we walked down Weston Lane, that when she was a girl, 'this was all fields' where she and her friends used to come to play. 'Yes Mum,' we would reply ('boring,' I would say under my breath!).

Moving on thirty-five years and, as anyone who's ever sat in the traffic at Weston Lane will tell you, how things have changed. Whole new industrial estates have shot up, factories have been built and retail outlets opened. Good for the town and employment I know, but it's funny how you don't really take notice at the time, of what you're losing.

Driving down Weston Lane with my two boys aged twelve and ten (note driving, not walking, another sign of the changes), it made me think of mum who passed away in 1988, just before my eldest son Greg was born. Before I knew it, I heard myself saying, just as mum did, 'when I was young...' only to be met by a resounding 'yeah Dad – boring!'

Crewe is, and always will be, home to me. But as my Crewe is so different from the place Mum must have known, I wonder what it will be like in another thirty-five years' time. Will my sons feel for the place the way I do now, or will they have taken their families and moved on, to find their own open fields?

Paul Aitken

The Magic Of Crewe in Yesteryears

A Crewe schoolboy's answer to Wembley Stadium and Lords rolled into one, was a stretch of waste land in the close proximity of Brierley Street, Thomas Street and Henry Street, known to the locals as 'The Razza'

Sketch of Smithy Cottage, as it looks today. The Duchy of Lancaster's estate offices in Old Park Lane, Weston Lane, Crewe.

The rear of property in Charles Street facing west from Wellington Street.

during the 1940s and '50s.

This was a magical patch of grassland, surrounded by souvenirs of the Second World War in the shape and form of both reinforced brick and metal, above and underground air-raid shelters; which locals fled to on hearing the sound of the warning sirens when the German Luftwaffe proposed to bomb Crewe Works and Rolls-Royce factories. Once the all-clear was given the boys would descend on The Razza looking for jagged lumps of shrapnel as souvenirs from the aftermath of the raid.

The Razza, without the benefit and luxury of any groundsman, was either void of grass, or overgrown with grass, dandelions and nettles. Yet in the summer it was the local

boys' Oval. In the winter months, without the luxury of goalposts and nets or stands, but with the goalkeepers standing between two piles of coats it was their very own Gresty Road.

These were hard times, when the leather-cased laced ball's bladder was punctured, it was miraculously replaced, with a pig's bladder dripping with blood obtained from the nearest slaughter house.

The players didn't possess the luxury of a football strip, instead they played in their school clothing, or in their factory overalls, unlike today's named and numbered shirts and shorts.

'Rolly' Sears, 'Pudgie' Evans, 'Chudah' Baker, Georgie Reeves, Ronnie Cope (son of Congleton Town FC's 'Killer' Cope), Kenny (Shunter) Roberts, Reg Tarporley were names that fifty years on easily spring to mind. Particularly Cope, who after the tragic Munich air disaster went on to star with Manchester United FC and Luton Town FC. Also, 'Shunter' Roberts, who later starred on the wing for Aston Villa FC. Sadly in those days Crewe Alexandra FC had talent scouts that were more blinkered than Red Rum, missing so much talent displayed under their noses on The Razza.

After the hard-fought games with any and every match being treated like a cup tie, we would all troop off sweaty and happy to one of Crewe's many cinemas. These were the good old days of the Empire, Kino, Odeon, Palace and the Plaza, not to mention the Lyceum Theatre.

Money was tight so we would all chip in and toss a coin to see who went up to the pay box and paid to get in. His responsibility was to make a beeline for the men's toilets and lift up the exit bars and hey presto, the gang were in!

In the heat of the summer we would think nothing of hiking to Church Minshull to swim in the canal or river, this being the free alternative to Crewe's public swimming baths in Flag Lane.

I have fond memories of Crewe people and neighbours who, unlike some today, cared about the community in the days of rationing during and shortly after the Second World War. I remember queuing at

Crewe Hall.

the shops with my mates after the Second World War for the first tins of salmon and fruit and packets of rice, which we'd not seen since 1939. We carried home our purchases with more joy and happiness than if we'd just won and were proudly exhibiting the FA Cup.

For Mother's Day we'd all go to the fields in Weston Lane, collecting bluebells whilst enjoying the freedom of the countryside. Sadly today, the green fields have vanished, 'swallowed up' by factories.

As a choirboy, I used to sing in the St Paul's church choir at Hightown. The caretaker used to treat this house of God with the care and reverence it deserved and merited. Today this once proud church stands empty of pews and is used as a furniture warehouse.

Every Sunday morning, I remember walking along Hungerford Road, taking a short-cut past Crewe railway station with my father to Cullen Street, (off Nantwich Road) to see my grandparents. When the front door opened, the aroma of home baking filled our nostrils. Grandma would open the doors of her black stove which had shiny brass handles and take out home-made apple and mince pies. With a hefty piece of pie on our plates and a cup of tea in our knees, Granddad would tell stories of his life as a guard on the Great Western Railway.

Evan Williams

CHAPTER 5
Sporting Crewe

Jeff Tudor (president of Crewe Wheelers Club) takes to the road for a 90-mile ride in the South Lancashire 100 race.

Crewe Wheelers hobo run to Middlewich.

My First Football Match

It was the 1957-58 season, and I was becoming interested in football. I had been listening to the scores on *Sports Report*, which was on the wireless every Saturday evening at five o'clock. This was a programme not to be missed by anyone with football interests; I was glued to the wireless so as not to miss a score as the announcer read them out.

I can remember my dad saying 'be quiet' as the scores were read out. He wrote them down in the column provided by the national newspaper. Then he checked is coupon hoping that he would have eight score draws (as was done the length and breath of the country) if this was the case he might be a very rich man.

It was Christmas Day and after opening my presents, I decided to go and watch Crewe Alexandra, which was my local Football League team. As I recall, they were playing Accrington Stanley and it was an eleven o'clock kick-off.

Never having been to a football league match before although it was a cold winter's day, I set off for the game. I knew where the ground was having seen the full address in the *News of The World Football Annual* which I bought before the season began.

The football ground was around one mile away. In those days people couldn't afford cars or bus fares or even pushbikes for their children, because money was hard-earned. My parents were not very well off, but we always had food on the table and an excellent Sunday lunch.

I set about walking to the ground with the money from aunts and uncles, which I received as Christmas presents. The walk was not too bad, as it helped to keep me warm on that cold winter's day.

The nearer I approached the ground the more excited I became, wondering what I was going to see at my first encounter with Crewe Alexandra in Division Three (North) and the Football League.

When I got to the ground I just followed the crowds who were going in to the popular side. I joined the queue for the children. As I recall, it was 3d to enter the ground and 1d for a programme.

The ground at Crewe Alexandra was very basic in the early days. There was the popular side where everybody stood up, the only seating was in the main wooden stand opposite the popular side which consisted of wooden forms with a number stamped on it – this was where you sat.

The Railway End of the ground had a little bit of terracing, then as you moved backwards up the terracing you had to stand on soil – there was no cover from the weather.

The Gresty Road End had no terracing at all, there was a slight incline which was all soil compacted down throughout the years and there was a roof which sheltered you from the weather. Crewe Alexandra won 4-1, and I can remember, Eddie McMorran an ex-Irish international scoring one of the best goals I have ever seen. He volleyed the ball up then hit it with is left foot, it went like a rocket straight into the top corner of the net – the goalkeeper never moved, it was unstoppable. As a coincidence, I was there on 2 March 1962 when Accrington Stanley played their last game in the Football League. It was played in a snowstorm at Crewe Alexandra's ground and Crewe won the game 4-0. Accrington Stanley football club was closed a few days later with debts of £60,000 and without

finishing their fixtures for the rest of the season.

After the first game I saw my mind was made up, the bug was starting to bite, I must go and see the remaining games for the rest of the season.

Over the years, I was to become a fanatic wherever Crewe Alexandra was concerned. My mates and I would even change our holidays, if they clashed with the fixtures of Crewe Alexandra, so we would never miss a game!

Ted Tunstall

Crewe's Football Referees

Isaac 'Ike' Baker

When he was a young man Isaac 'Ike' Baker first started playing football for Shavington, and he soon made a name for himself playing in the outside-right position. He then moved from Shavington to Nantwich, where he played for one and a half seasons, eventually moving to Coppenhall. The season after he joined them Coppenhall won the Crewe League and five cups that included *The Sentinel* trophy.

He progressed to refereeing his first match at the Barony, Nantwich, in charge of two school teams. After the match he was presented with 9d as his reward for refereeing the match. He continued to work his way up the refereeing ladder via the Crewe and District League, the Combination League, the Birmingham League and finally to the English Football League where he officiated for seventeen years in all aspects of first-class football.

With his knowledge of refereeing, having had twenty-five years of experience, 'Ike'

The Cup Final in 1926 at Wembley Stadium.

class matches, which also included one international game, four Inter-League games, five finals and two semi-finals.

He was the third referee from Crewe to receive the highest honour a referee could receive: officiating at the English Cup Final between Bolton Wanderers and Manchester City at Wembley Stadium, on 24 April 1926.

After he retired he continued in football and travelled around different football grounds working as a talent scout for Aston Villa Football Club.

Alfred Baker – Football League Referee

Following in the footsteps, or rather bootsteps, of his father Alfred Baker aged fifteen years started refereeing in a junior football game. At the age of twenty-one he was elected to the Central League panel, then the Birmingham League until in 1939 he was appointed to the English League panel. He refereed practically all the leading club games in the First and Second Divisions, officiating in over 250 games in both England and Ireland.

The highlights of his career included refereeing the Welsh Cup Final in 1925 at Wrexham, performing as a linesman at the English Football League Cup Final at Wolverhampton (Wolverhampton Wanderers *v.* Sunderland) in 1942 and, at Stoke, refereeing the FA XI *v.* Army XI in 1944. He was in line to follow his father and be appointed in charge of the FA Cup Final, when he suffered from a recurring knee injury and was forced to retire from active football in 1948.

However, he will be remembered most for the match he refereed in 1946. The match was a Third Division (North) Cup game played at Edgeley Park, Stockport, between Stockport County and Doncaster Rovers on

officiated in a great range and number of matches. These include: Antrim Shield; Belfast City Cup; Cheshire Cup (2); Hallamshire Cup (2); Hull City Hospital Cup; Irish Cup (3); Irish Gold Cup; Lincolnshire Cup; Llandiloes Cup; London Challenge Cup; Northampton Shield (3); Montgomery Cup (6); Staffordshire Cup (2); Welsh Cup (2); Inter-League games; five International games and numerous minor competitions. (Numbers in brackets denote frequency of appearance)

On two separate occasions he officiated in the London Cup semi-finals and in the 1911-12 season he refereed the English Cup semi-final played at Liverpool between Blackburn Rovers and West Bromwich Albion. His busiest season was in the 1911-12 season when he officiated in sixty first-

He was forced to retire at the age of forty due to a recurring knee injury.

Elected to the Central League Panel of referees aged twenty-one in 1928.

Saturday, 30 March 1946. At the end of ninety minutes' play the score was 2-2, and the rules of the competition were that ten minutes' extra time each way was to be played. At the end of extra time there was still no winner so the referee took the players off the football pitch for consultation and spectators then started to leave the ground thinking that the game was finished. However, the referee explained to both teams that the rules also stated that at this juncture in a game they had to play on until a deciding result was achieved. The teams went back on to the pitch whereupon spectators who were leaving, thinking that it was all over, started to go back into the ground to watch the continuation of this struggle. Some spectators who lived in the vicinity of the football ground went home, had their tea and returned to watch the match. The game continued with players from both sides, and the referee, showing signs of exhaustion. In the ninety-third minute of the second period of extra time, when the referee consulted his linesmen all three agreed that due to bad light (this was not helped by smoke from the nearby locomotive shed) the game would have to stop. This mammoth game was all the more remarkable bearing in mind that three Doncaster players (Swallow, Marriott and Jordan) had worked a night shift the day before the match and that another Doncaster player, Stirland, was suffering from influenza and pleurisy! The referee was amongst one of the many casualties needing treatment for cramp. The total time the teams played was for 203 minutes (this was made up of ninety minutes' normal time, twenty minutes' extra time and then ninety-three minutes without an interval). This is the longest continuously played football game recorded in this country. A crowd of 12,730 spectators paid £1,023 18s 6d to watch this historic match being played and the referee and linesmen were paid the princely sum of £5 5s 6d between them for their services.

When he retired Alfred Baker continued to emulate his father and also visited different football grounds working as a talent scout for Aston Villa FC. He was also involved for many years with the Crewe and District Football League.

Mr D.A. Baker

Local Cricket

From the discovery of an 1889 membership card we learn that The Crewe (LNWR) Cricket Club was established in 1850 when Crewe town was still in its infancy.

The club's field, in 1889, was pleasantly situated on the old Wistaston Road (now Stewart Street) near the Rockwood Inn. At that time it would have been possible to see from the ground across the fields as far as Walthall Street.

Membership subscriptions at that time were 6s per annum for adults and 4s for apprentices. This was quite a tidy sum when one considers that, twenty-three years later, in 1912, the London and North Western Railway Company only paid £1 7s 6d per week to their Permanent Way Gangers. This could indicate that, at the time, playing cricket was a sport enjoyed only by the upper echelons of the railway workforce.

Alderman Francis W. Webb JP was the club president and the patrons included the Chairman (Sir Richard Moon, Bart) and the Directors of the LNWR. The club Secretary

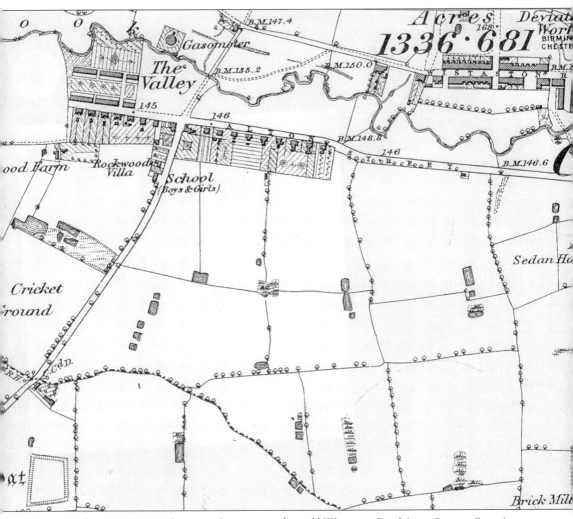

A map of where LNWR Cricket ground was situated on old Wistaston Road (now Stewart Street).

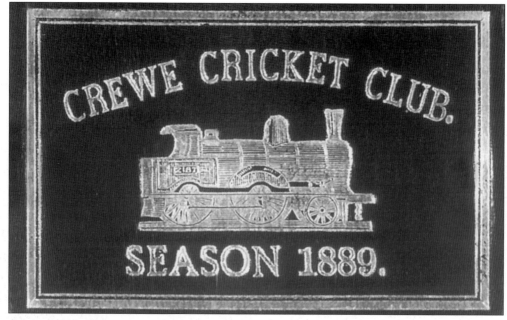

Crewe Cricket Club, season ticket for the year 1889.

was J. Nixon of No. 21 Wistaston Road.

The attractive black leather-bound membership card, heavily embossed in gold lettering, shows a 2-4-0 locomotive number 2187. This particular engine appears to be more emblematic than representational as its name was *Penrith Beacon* seemingly not connected with cricket at all. Probably it was shown as a tribute to the designer, their President, Alderman F.W. Webb. The membership card was printed by Henry Taylor of Crewe. That year the club had fixtures with Runcorn, Wolverhampton, Wistaston, Bunbury, Nantwich, Calveley, Porthill, Audlem, Lawton and Davenham.

The Crewe Cricket Club subsequently moved their home to the Alexandra Stadium in Earle Street, where in the 1930s local derby matches with Nantwich regularly attracted crowds of 4,000. Most of the supporters from Nantwich had to walk to Earle Street in those days to see the match.

One notable bowling achievement was set at the Earle Street ground in 1922 when Fred Sylvester took nine wickets for nine runs. Fred's son Jack, now eighty-eight years old, still has the ball, which is kept on a stand. Its engraved plate has almost been worn away after so many years of proud polishing.

When the Earle Street Ground was sold in the late 1960s the Crewe Cricket Club moved to Willaston where they still play fine cricket keeping up the name of this 152-year-old club.

Brian Edge

Crewe Works 10 Shop Cricket Final Winners 1950, at Goddard Street playing field.

Gerald Clowes, best all rounder at the Crewe Wheelers Club. Back row, from left to right: Ken Bennion, Peter Robinson, Eric Carless, Jeff Tudor, Albert Clowes, John Bratby. Front row, from left to right: Pat O'Keefe, John Gallimore, Gerald Clowes, Dennis Reed (from the Evening Sentinel) and Brian Evans.

Western Sports Club in 1970. Jeff Tudor takes the winners trophy in the CIU Presidents Final, Dave Kelly was the runner-up.

Permanent Way Bowling Presentation in 1968.

Members of the Hop Pole public house A and B bowls teams, who both reached the final of the John Davies South Cheshire League knock-out in 1973. The final should have been played on neutral ground but it was agreed they could stage the match on their home green on this occasion and the A team were triumphant.

CHAPTER 6

Nantwich People

Vin and Kathleen Armstrong on their wedding day in 1956.

Churches Mansion where in the 1950s you could hold your wedding reception for only 8s 6d per head.

Home Town Childhood Memories

I always said, 'I will return to Nantwich one day', where else?

I was born in 1935 in Welsh Row, Nantwich. Ours was a tiny black and white cottage, two up and two down, with an outside lavatory and a long back garden. All for 2s 6d a week.

As a small child, we moved to Hawthorn Avenue, off Crewe Road: a row of Victorian cottages, twenty-three in all. There I stayed until I was married.

I went to Manor Road school, starting in the infants and finishing at fifteen in the seniors, all on the same site.

I met Vin, my future husband, when we were very young and married at twenty-one, in the beautiful parish church of St Mary's, with its wonderful stained glass windows and carved choir stalls. Our wedding reception was held in Churches Mansion; a roast turkey lunch with trifle to follow, only 8s 6d per head!

Vin was a police constable and after our wedding we moved away from Nantwich. The police were moved around Cheshire frequently then and we lived in a number of places. I always knew I would return to Nantwich one day, back to my routes.

My mother's family all came from First Wood Street, in many ways the place most dear to my heart. First Wood Street, as I remember it, was a small street with houses on each side. Front doors opened onto the cobbled street, the back doors opened almost into the River Weaver! All had an outside toilet and shared a back yard. They were two up, two down, with a pantry.

During school holidays I went to First Wood Street on most days. There I played with cousins and friends. Our games were played mainly on the riverbank: skipping; tick; top and whip and hopscotch. When the weather warmed up, we paddled in the river; girls with cotton dresses tucked into their knickers. We fished for tiddlers using jam jars, and swung across the river hanging onto low lying branches. The riverbank was lined with trees and we would pinch apples from the gardener's orchard which backed on to the river. Sometimes he chased us and we dropped the apples as we made our escape!

On 5 November we always had a bonfire on the riverbank. Fireworks too if someone managed to get some. Friends and neighbours gathered together and roasted potatoes and chestnuts. I vaguely remember a VE party in the street; a trestle table, paper hats, flags and Jamey faces.

Other times we played in Nana's shared yard, giving concerts for neighbours who were interested, dressing up in old curtains and high heeled shoes – old ones, of course, found in someone's cupboard.

Sir Edmund Wright Almshouses. They were built in 1634 and are seen here in 1974 in London Road, Nantwich, before being dismantled and rebuilt in Beam Street in 1975. They now form part of a senior citizens' home.

During summer holidays out came the old rusty bikes and off we would go – at least ten of us – a motley crowd! Roads were safe then with very little traffic. Up Welsh Row and into Marsh Lane we went, taking bottles of water and a few sandwiches. We were off for the day! Happy carefree days. Stopping to refresh ourselves, we'd sit in the grass making daisy chains and looking for a four-leafed clover. It didn't seem to rain, or maybe we didn't notice!

Delucci's ice cream cart came round summer and winter. We waited on the corner of the street, each clutching 3d, for the brightly painted cart to appear. Mrs Delucci was dark-haired and dark-eyed with long flashing earrings. Clanging a large school bell she drew up the horse and we flocked around the cart. The horse patiently waited as the customers were served, then off it clattered further in to Welsh Row.

There were few shops around First Wood Street, and the Three Pigeons public house yard backed on to the street. Bellfields antique shop was situated at the top of the street. The shop front was on Welsh Row. On the opposite side from Bellfields was Silcock dairy shop. The herbalist and Vimto bar was on the corner. Mr Davies, the owner, was a small, dark, sallow, thin man, perpetually smoking a cigarette. As he spoke, the cigarette clung

The old mill, which stood in Mill Street, Nantwich, viewed from Welsh Row in 1966. The mill was destroyed by fire in the 1970s.

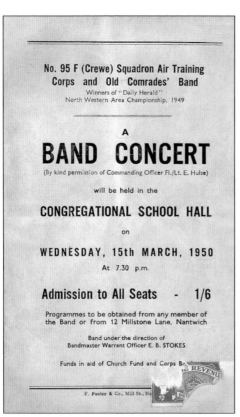

Band Concert programme from 1950.

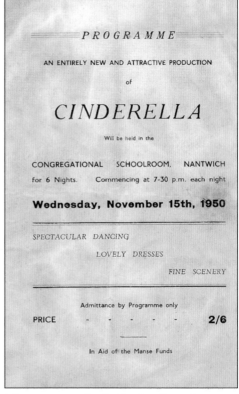

The programme for the Cinderella performance.

The cast of Cinderella, *in which Kathleen Armstrong played the lead role.*

to his lips and we thought it was a magic trick! There were chairs and tables scattered around. People met to play cards and drink Vimto and so did we, when we had 4d in our pockets. Next door on Welsh Row, Mr and Mrs Dentith had their small shop, selling sweets and a few groceries. The couple stood behind their scrubbed counter wearing long white aprons, almost touching the floor. We called in to buy sweets, weighed on shining scales using tiny weights then poured into cone shaped bags. Heath's shop came next, a real Aladdin's cave. It was dark and musty, I loved it! Full of toys and novelties for 3d and 6d. We bought packets of tiny coloured beads, complete with needle and thread, only to break when made into a necklace, beads everywhere, me probably

in tears. Tops and whips, skipping ropes, cars, boats, marbles, all jumbled together in dusty boxes.

Our playing didn't extend further on this side, not past the Widow's Almshouses (Cheshire Cat) on the other side of the street. These houses were blocked and derelict and people said they were haunted!

An odd couple, hardly ever seen, lived just past the Three Pigeons. We called the old man 'Pom-pom', why I don't know. Outside their house was a man-hole cover. We jumped up and down on it and the noise was deafening. The old man came out, shaking his fists, waving his arms about and we all ran away. Thoughtless of us. Eventually the old couple died and people moved in to clear the house. Rumour had it

A scene from Cinderella.

that they had to wear masks over their noses and mouths while doing this.

Time passed and I went to First Wood Street less often to play, but I still went to visit grandparents and other relatives. I started to play with Jean who lived next door to me in Hawthorn Avenue. Jean and I became bosom pals and went everywhere together. We used to sit on a wooden gate frame at the bottom of Laburnum Avenue, facing Crewe Road, until our bottoms were numb, watching the world go by, not many cars, but quite a lot of green double-decker buses going to Willaston and Crewe.

The rag and bone man came round now and then, shouting, 'Rag a' bone', in a raucous voice. Into our houses we ran, pleading for old rags, enough for a windmill or a balloon. My mother would have preferred a cup and saucer. The ragman also came with a horse and cart; the cart was a jumble of rags, windmills, balloons, cups and saucers, not Wedgwood or Doulton, I hasten to add!

All of the houses in Hawthorn Avenue had a small front garden and a tiny yard. We sometimes played in Jean's yard, not ours, as my father kept racing pigeons. These were housed in a cote that took up most of the yard. The atmosphere in our house was full of tension on racing days, almost unbearable! Dad, pacing up and down, tin of corn, waiting for the birds to arrive back. We couldn't use our outside lavatory on these days in case we disturbed the pigeons, 'when landing'. Instead, we had to sprint to my auntie's house; she lived at the top of the avenue.

My dad was a member of The White Horse (Pillory Street) flying club. One of his birds, which we called Red Shadow, was proved to be the best in the club. We had a

Nantwich High Street in 1972 when traffic was still moving in both directions. The whole area is now pedestrianized.

picture, hanging in the house, of this pigeon. Pigeon racing was a popular pastime in those days.

Outside No. 15 Hawthorn Avenue stood a gas lamp. A man came at dawn and dusk to light and extinguish it. He came on his bike carrying a long pole. It was time for us to go in after the lighting.

Jean and I would go to the pictures, the Regal and the Cosy. The Regal is now Chatwins bakery, and the Cosy, Gregory's nightclub. Saturday night was the highlight of the week: going to the pictures, and chips on the way home! About this time we started to go to social evenings held in the Congregational school hall, situated in Monks Lane, now prestigious town houses. Here we went to Sunday School and sang on the Anniversary platform. Our mothers usually made us a pretty dress to wear. Most women worked in one of the sewing factories in Nantwich – all gone now! We always had a yearly outing with Sunday school, usually to Rhyl or New Brighton.

When I was about fifteen, I sang in a Band Concert, held in the Congregational school hall, wearing a long, pink, taffeta dress. I really felt grown up. About this time, Mr Cross, a church member, started to produce pantomimes. I remember playing Cinderella; the excitement was wonderful, peeping through the curtains on opening

The fire engine that Robert Davies's dad drove, leaves the depot at Beam Street, Nantwich, on a call.

night to see if we knew anyone in the audience – butterflies in the stomach as the opening bars of music were played. Mothers sewed some costumes, some we hired and a lady came to make up our faces. The 'Congregational' was an all-important place to me.

As we moved in to our teens, Jean and I went to Saturday night dances in Crewe to a place called The Studio in Mill Street. It was the 'in' place then. We went by bus and nearly missed the last one home quite often!

Then I met Vin and my 'acting' days were over. We walked, went to the pictures and weekly dances held in the Civic Hall. Vin did National Service at eighteen, and soon after he returned from Hong Kong, we were married.

Some twenty years on, we moved to Bridgemere, seven miles from Nantwich. I go into Nantwich often during the week and find the old town changed, with its now bustling streets, busy roads and many more houses. Snow Hill, once a hill literally, is now a car park, Wood Street too. No one paddles in the river anymore.

I meet friends from the past, which I enjoy. Nantwich, despite all the change will always be very special to me. Some nights I lie awake and travel, in my mind, through the old streets as I remember them; it feels good.

Kathleen Armstrong

Nantwich Firefighter

'Follow us...it's at your house!'

'Quick, wake up, Robert. Get out of bed, the house is on fire!'

Not really how a ten-year-old boy expects to be roused from a deep sleep – especially when his father happens to be a local part-time fireman.

Our house was on the Barony Road in Nantwich and I lived there with my parents, Hilda and Ivor Davies. Dad worked at Harvey's Tannery in Millstone Lane, now a housing estate, and like many of the local employers, the Tannery allowed their firemen employees to leave work immediately when summoned for fire emergencies.

In those pre-mobile phone days, the alarm was raised by means of a siren, which could be heard all over town. At night, however, the siren could not be used so each fireman's house was fitted with a bell. Ours was by the stairs and to this day, I can vividly remember the tremendous racket it made when it woke us and the neighbours!

On this eventful morning, as I swung my legs out of bed I could smell smoke and, hearing the wail of the siren in the distance, I realized that Mum had already called the fire brigade.

As it happens, the house was not on fire but the chimney was – or to be precise, the soot in the chimney was on fire. At this time chimney fires occurred very frequently as most people still had coal fires and this became the most common reason for calling out the brigade.

It suddenly dawned on me that Dad had already left for work so it shouldn't be long before he would be returning home, this time driving the fire engine.

However, one of the problems at the Tannery was that, because of the noise, it was often difficult to hear the sound of the siren and that is precisely what happened on this particular morning. Dad did not hear the siren but fortunately one of his friends working outside rushed in to tell him that it was sounding.

One thing all the firemen prided themselves on was their ability to get to the station as quickly as possible and there was plenty of competition to see who could get there first to man the fire engine.

In the 1950s, very few members of the brigade owned cars. It was a very common sight to see them cycling from all directions of the town to the fire station (then situated on the opposite side of Beam Street to the present fire station on the site of today's Lady Helen Walk).

On this particular day, Dad soon realized that because of the delay in hearing the siren he would probably not reach the station before the engine left, but pressed on cycling along Millstone Lane and turned left into Beam Street only to see the fire engine racing towards him. He expected a toot on the horn and a wave from his colleagues, which was the usual routine. To his amazement, the engine slowed right down and one of the firemen wound down the window and shouted, 'Turn around and follow us – it's at your house!'.

I'm surprised he managed to stay on his bicycle but, having recovered from the shock, he set off after the fire engine pedalling furiously, rather like a character from the *Keystone Cops*.

You can imagine the reception that awaited him at our house. Fortunately, the chimney was dealt with and there was very little damage but Dad was not allowed to forget the incident for many years to come and from that day on the chimney sweep was a regular visitor to our house.

My Dad died in 1994 and he would have been proud of the fact that the modern day fire fighters of Nantwich honoured his twenty-three years' service in the brigade by their presence at his funeral in St Mary's church, Nantwich, some serving as pallbearers.

R.J. Davies

Happy Days At The Cottage

I started working for the Health Service in the 1960s and my 'career' began in the hospital kitchens at the Barony, right at the bottom as a kitchen porter. Within a short time I was lucky enough to fulfil my ambition and get taken on as a trainee in theatre, working at the Crewe Memorial hospital, studying for and passing several City and Guilds exams in theatre work and becoming a member of the Institute of Theatre Technicians. By 1971 the new Leighton Hospital was due to open, and extra theatre personnel had been taken on to staff the sixteen operating theatres which would eventually be in action once the new hospital was up and running. In the meantime we had far too many staff for the two theatres at Crewe Memorial so other jobs and activities had to be found to keep us out of mischief. One of these was at Nantwich Cottage hospital, a small establishment which dealt with minor operations and the like, presided over with meticulous attention to detail by Matron Duncalfe.

My own memories of Nantwich Cottage are mixed. My first meeting with Matron Duncalfe was not auspicious. She ran the place like a training camp, she being the Camp Commandant. On my first morning there I parked my car and went boldly in through the front door. Half way down the entrance hall a voice barked from a side office, 'Who are you and where do you think you are going?' I froze. This must be the voice of Matron Duncalfe. A small tubby lady appeared at the office door.

She eyed me up and down and made me feel like I'm about to go on parade in the army.

'I'm Roy Butler, one of the technicians from Memorial Hospital, come to work in your operating theatre'. I hardly dared look her in the eye.

'Are you?' she replied, 'well, when you are working in my hospital you will follow my rules, the first one is you do not park your car there, you take it round the back and put it out of sight. The second rule is you do not enter this hospital by the front door. You will use the tradesmen's entrance, and please don't forget it. The front door is for Consultants only.' So ended my first lesson. I retreated rapidly out of the building with my tail between my legs.

Only minor operations were carried out at the cottage hospital. The building was converted from a large house, and had six female beds, six male beds, and four beds for children. For the patients it was the nearest you could get to being ill in your own home. The food was excellent. All the other hospitals in the South Cheshire group had to order their food stocks straight from headquarters at the Barony, but Matron Duncalfe did not comply with this arrangement. Her supplies came straight from local shops in Nantwich and when they were delivered each morning she inspected them herself. If they were not good enough for her to pass her eagle eye, then the offending articles were returned to the supplier with a note pointing out that if he offered supplies like this again the hospital would not ask him to supply any more goods in future. All the baking and cooking was done on an Aga. The lady in charge in the kitchen was a mistress of her art and every morning the aroma drifting round the hospital from the kitchen was delicious.

Very often grateful patients would leave presents for the staff such as a tin of biscuits, a basket of fruit, tins of sweets and bottles of wine. When this happened, these were not locked away for senior staff, but made available to all, they were left on show on a large sideboard in the staff dining room and when you had finished your meal you could help yourself to anything you fancied. I always admired Matron Duncalfe for that. In other hospitals where I worked, the staff at the lower end of the scale saw very little of what patients and relatives left for employees.

However, Matron Duncalfe could have come straight out of a 'Carry On' film. I heard her give a telling off to a patient because he was going to the toilet and the top three buttons of his pyjama jacket were undone.

'How dare you walk about this hospital in such an untidy state, do your jacket up man. I will not have my young nurses being exposed to such behaviour.' The poor patient shuffled back to his bed muttering to himself, 'Bloody hell, I think she must have trained the Gestapo Officers during the war,' he whispered to the chap in the next bed. 'Yes,' he responded, 'she's a tough old bird, but her

heart is in the right place.' The poor chap fastened his offending buttons and tried again to go for a wee. Another patient came in for a ticking off because he hadn't eaten his watercress, which had been served with salmon and salad. He had cleared his plate but had left the watercress on the side. Matron happened to spot this and insisted that the leaves of watercress be eaten completely. 'But I don't like the stuff,' argued the patient, 'I never eat it at home.' 'I don't care what you do at home', she replied 'you are in my care now and you will do as I ask.' She was such a powerful and domineering person that the patient sat down and did as he was told just like a child.

One morning I arrived at the Cottage to find the place was buzzing with gossip. When I had prepared the theatre ready for the morning's list one of the young nurses told me what all the chat was about.

This is what had happened. During visiting hours on the previous evening, most of the patients had visitors with them and the nurses on the evening shift took the opportunity to have a chat and a cup tea in the staff room. The scene was normal enough, patients and visitors talking quietly between themselves, nurses talking about the events of the day.

Slowly the chatter died away and people became aware of some moaning and groaning coming from a private room, which contained a lady who was a private patient.

'What is the matter with the patient in the private room? She seems to be in some discomfort,' remarked the senior nurse. Turning to the junior nurse on duty she asked her to go and find out what was the matter.

'Yes sister,' and off went the junior

The Cottage Hospital, Nantwich.

nurse. All this time the sounds of distress had got noticeably louder and everyone was quite concerned. The young nurse tapped gently on the door and waited, but got no response. After a polite pause during which the moaning reached a fever pitch, the young nurse tapped loudly on the door and without waiting for a response walked straight in. When she saw what was going on, her bottom jaw dropped to her shoes and her face went bright red. She turned on her heel, shut the door quietly behind her and went back to the staff room.

The groaning did not stop. In fact it grew louder. 'What on earth is going on in that room?' asked the sister. The young nurse was speechless. 'Nurse, what is going on in that room, will you tell me what's happening?' The young nurse was so embarrassed she could not get the words out.

Eventually she managed to splutter, 'They're having it off.' 'Having it off. What do you mean, having it off?' But the nurse was helpless with laughter and couldn't answer the question. The senior nurse (a spinster) turned to the rest of staff in the room and asked them, 'What does this mean, having it off? Does she mean they are drinking in there?' By now the rest of the staff were helpless with laughter and couldn't speak properly, the visitors and other patients had also got wind of what was going on, having overheard the senior nurse. They were all

106

in tucks as well. Finally the moaning stopped and sanity slowly took over. 'I shall go and see for myself what is going on in that room,' barked the senior nurse. 'No, please don't do that,' said another member of the staff. 'You might be a little embarrassed by what you see.' 'Me, embarrassed? After thirty years working in hospitals I think I have seen all there is to see.' 'Well, you know, they were doing it, having sex,' explained the young nurse.

'What. Doing what? Doing that in my hospital?' 'Well,' said one of the others, 'it's surprising what you can get on the National Health Service these days.'

I never did find out what Matron Duncalfe's reaction was when she read about these goings on in the Ward Report the following morning. If visiting the toilet with the top button undone on your pyjama jacket merits a serious reprimand, goodness only knows what punishment was meted out for putting a hospital bed through such unnecessary trauma!

Roy Butler

CHAPTER 7

Surrounding Villages

Betley Street, Crewe, with its enduring memories of the 'old railway village'.

Betley

Betley Court Railway

'Gaffers Row' (intended for works' foremen) remains in Victoria Street and, in the heart of the town, there are three delightful terraces hidden away behind iron gates at the end of the street. Here, residents say the community spirit of a village persists to this day. In the centre of this 'village' is Betley Street.

In the village that had given the street its name events proceeded at a more leisurely pace. Whereas in Crewe development depended on the railway, in Betley it depended on two estate owners, the Tollets in the north end of the village and the Twemlows in the south. While in Crewe the London North Western Rail Company (LNWR) built an engineering plant, houses, schools, public baths and even churches, George Tollet of Betley Hall was busy with his model farm (now Old Hall) and Francis Twemlow was chairman of the Staffordshire Quarter Sessions, as well as being a director of the 'Knotty' (North Staffordshire Railway Company). Apart from building the home farm, Francis Twemlow made no significant alterations or improvements to either the house or the village. In this respect he differed from his son Thomas, who on coming into the estate proceeded to build the clock tower and stable block and to build or remodel many of the estate's houses in the village which to this day bear his initials, T.F.T. This achievement was outmatched in Crewe in 1887 by LNWR's gift to the town (to commemorate the jubilee of the Queen and the railway!) of splendid Queen's Park.

My family and I now live in Betley Court and have done for twenty-three years. The house was built for John Cradock, an attorney at law from a Cheshire family, in 1716. We have done our best to restore a near derelict property where William Emes laid out the garden in 1785 and where John Nash remodelled the drawing room in 1809.

When in 1996 the potteries celebrated the 150th anniversary of the foundation Knotty, it seemed wrong that Betley Court should not mark the occasion in some way. After all Francis Twemlow had been a principle progenitor of the railway, yet no trace remained of the many years he had lived in the house. So, stimulated by our growing family of grandchildren and a fortuitous auction purchase, Freda, my wife, and I decide to install a garden railway as the house's own 'Knotty'. We were able to tuck away a miniature 5in gauge railway in a rather disregarded corner of the garden where it is almost hidden by greenery. It reproduces schematically the Knotty line from Crewe to Hare Castle with stations at Radway Green, Alsager and Lawton. There are branch lines to Mow Cop and to Sandbach. Crewe station is of course the largest of the stations and doubles up as an engine shed! Su Hurrell, the artist, has caught the spirit of the 'Betley Court Railway' in her pictorial map. The railway gives the family much pleasure. At least in Betley's Crewe station it doesn't matter if the train is late!

When Francis Twemlow died in 1865 the local paper carried a very long tribute to his work for the area, and ended with a grandiloquent flourish:

'Distinguished in public usefulness up to a

FRANCIS TWEMLOW, OF BETLEY COURT.

Francis Twemlow of Betley Court, whose foresight stimulated railway progress.

Harecastle Station with Francis Twemlow's Betley Court Farm in the background.

Queen's Park, Crewe showing the clock tower paid for by the LNWR workforce in appreciation of their director's generosity in giving the park to the town to mark the jubilee of both the Queen and the company.

The man-made boat lake in Queen's Park, which has given pleasure to generations of people over the years. Today the 45-acre park is considered one of the finest in the country.

Francis Twemlow's son, Thomas, built this clock tower (now The Clockhouse) and stable block in 1870. The building in the foreground is Betley Court's seventeenth-century dove-house.

few years before his death. Spending those last few years in the quiet of his rural home, the sun of his life has set peacefully and calmly. It was impossible to wish for anyone a more desirable exit from the stage of life than that permitted to him whose life has ebbed away under the shadow of the great trees that flank Betley Court.'

Those same trees now canopy an unusual but appropriate memorial to a business pioneer of the railways.

Betley Street, Crewe and Crewe station, Betley illustrate the changes that nearly two centuries of railway history have made to the lives of the people in this area. Crewe has grown from virtually nothing into a major industrial town at the centre of communications. Today its station is used by a number of different railways just as it was in the nineteenth century, and it is a shopping centre, with its own market, to which people from much older surrounding villages like Betley travel, often on a weekly basis. Betley has lost its market and indeed its station, Betley Road, (1875-1945: passengers; 1963: goods) yet remains a pleasant place to live and welcomes visitors from Crewe and elsewhere. Recently it has become a magnet for developers. Hopefully, unlike Betley Street 'village', it will not become an historic enclave surrounded by modern buildings.

Godfrey N. Brown

112

Betley Court. The central gate with its gilded inter-linked initials commemorates John Craddock's marriage to Anastasia Abnett of Audley in 1722.

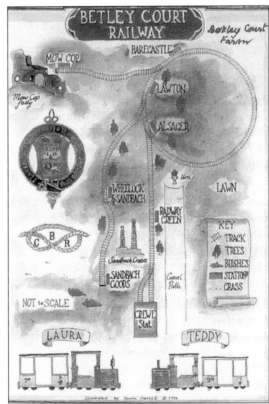

Su Hurrell's map of Betley Court Railway.

A poster from Crewe Station.

Crewe Station, Betley, displays a nineteenth-century timetable for the line.

Bunbury

'...When Knights Were Bold...'

It may seem strange that Bunbury, an ancient village roughly in the centre of the Cheshire plain, can boast of having three medieval knights who achieved international fame. In chronological order they were Sir Hugh Calveley, Sir Ralph Egerton and Sir George Beeston. Much is known about the careers of all three knights but tantalisingly, in all three cases, some important details are unknown. Some hundreds of years later, the only thing that can be said with absolute certainty, is that all three knights have imposing memorials in their parish church of St Boniface, Bunbury.

Sir Hugh Calveley was born in 1320. The family held the manor of Calveley, a township of Bunbury, since the time of King John. At one time Hugh Calveley led a free company of soldiers (in modern terms perhaps best described as mercenaries) in the Hundred Years War, and received his knighthood after success in Brittany in 1346.

Sir Hugh Calveley's reputation has survived the centuries being described as, 'A giant of a man, with projecting cheek bones, a receding hair line, red hair and long teeth'. He had a large appetite, eating as much as four men and drinking as much as ten. He was kind and chivalrous, honoured among men and of great strength. He was a religious man, whenever he siezed booty he had it

Tomb of Sir Hugh Calveley, Knight, who lived from 1320 to 1394.

sprinkled with Holy Water, to absolve him of his sins in taking it! In later life, he became a generous benefactor to Bunbury church.

Sir Hugh's connection with Bunbury church dates from 1385 when he purchased the rights to the church. Traditionally, Sir Hugh is credited with being the founder of the present Bunbury church, but architectural considerations suggest he adapted an existing stone church to his own needs, possibly to ease his way to heaven. After an adventurous and perhaps not entirely chivalrous career, he also founded and endowed a College at Bunbury in 1387. Sir Hugh's College remained until 1547 when it was dissolved by a statute of Edward VI.

Without doubt, Sir Hugh Calveley's association with Bunbury church has been remembered continuously since his death on 23 April 1394. Certainly every bride coming to the altar has detoured around Sir Hugh's magnificent tomb situated in the centre of the chancel. It is noteworthy that a chancel tomb location is usually assigned to none but a king, but maybe Sir Hugh, as 'owner' of Bunbury church thought he had a similar entitlement. The white alabaster effigy confirms his great stature and his claim to be 'The Giant of Bunbury'. Yet his tomb poses another puzzle concerning Sir Hugh Calveley, for it is uncertain even if Sir Hugh was ever buried at Bunbury. There is no evidence for or against, and the tomb may be merely a cenotaph. In an attempt to clarify this uncertainty the tomb was opened in 1848. According to J. Fenna, Churchwarden:

'I found the fragments of an oak coffin, apparently of uncommon size, almost crumbled to dust; the handles of the sides being iron were nearly entire. By the side of his coffin lay a lead coffin, quite fresh, with the initials D.M.C. that I suppose to be that of Dame Mary Calveley? I measured some of the bones which I have no doubt were Sir Hugh's, from their extraordinary size. The thighbone, was two inches or more larger than the average size of men. He is supposed to have measured seven feet six inches in height when he lived.'

Later historians confirmed that the bones were quite clearly those of Dame Mary Calveley and her husband Sir Hugh Calveley. Most of Sir Hugh Calveley's alterations beautified Bunbury church and remain visible to the present day.

The second of the Bunbury heroic knights is Sir Ralph Egerton of Ridley, who was the second son of Philip Egerton of Egerton. At the Battle of Tournay in 1513 Ralph Egerton distinguished himself by taking the French Standard. His royal master was very appreciative, for Ralph Egerton was knighted and appointed Standard Bearer of England for life at a salary of £100 per annum. Sir Ralph was also granted the Manor of Ridley, together with lands therein and in other places. Ridley Manor House was, in those days, a massive establishment transformed by a previous owner Sir William Stanley, into 'the finest

Close-up of Sir Hugh Calveley's tomb.

Memorial to Sir Ralph Egerton on display in St Boniface's church, Bunbury.

south side of the chancel. This chapel is usually, and perhaps confusingly, called the Ridley Chapel though it is sometimes more correctly referred to as the Egerton Chapel. The doorway retains its ancient wooden doors and hinges, with delicate monograms of Sir Ralph and his Lady Margaret.

Sir Ralph died on 4 March 1528 before his chantry chapel was completed. In his detailed will, he left precise instructions for completion of his chantry and also burial arrangements:

'He thereby orders his body to be buried in the chapel of Bunbury and that twelve torches be borne by twelve men in black gowns on the day of his burial and twenty-four tapers burning about his body the same day.'

The executors were also charged to erect a tomb for him with a large marble stone with his name and arms engraved and with this addition, 'the King's standard bearer and treasurer to the Lady Princess' and also a guilt plate fastened on the wall with his names and arms and additions as above. Sir Ralph also endowed a house in Bunbury for two chantry priests to pray for his soul, for his father's and mother's souls, and for all Christian souls forever. The Chantry House was to contain two chambers, one parlour, a buttery and a kitchen, and the said priests to be maintained out of his mills at Nantwich.

In 2001, Sir Ralph's chapel survives complete with his memorial plate. The images and his large marble tomb have, however, disappeared but a sandstone slab beneath the present-day blue carpet indicates the tomb location. The black and white house, still known as 'The

gentleman's house in all Cheshire'. In later times Ridley Manor was garrisoned by parliamentary troupes, surviving a Royalist attack in 1645, and was burnt down around 1700.

While Sir Ralph was undoubtedly a national hero he is best remembered locally for his close association with Bunbury church. During Sir Ralph's lifetime Bunbury Parish church also retained the college that had been founded by Sir Hugh Calveley. Possibly Sir Ralph wished to emulate Sir Hugh and attempt to ease his way to heaven by building a large chantry chapel on the

Print of the tomb of Sir George Beeston.

Chantry House', has been restored in the twentieth century as a private house, and is located about two hundred metres to the south of the church.

The third of the Bunbury knights, Sir George Beeston, was both a soldier and a sailor and is, perhaps, the most enigmatic of the three. He was born in 1499 but his life in earlier adult years seems unrecorded. Sir George, although a soldier, laid his principle claim to fame as a sailor. He fought with Drake, Frobisher and Hawkins against the Spanish Armada. For his part in the battle against the Armada, George Beeston was knighted on board the 'Arc', at sea, by the Lord High Admiral, Lord Howard of Effingham. Even though the story of the Armada is remarkable, even more remarkable is that Sir George Beeston was reputed to have been eighty-nine years old at the time! Little is known about Sir George Beeston's ship, the *Dreadnought*, which was built in 1573. Her displacement was 400 tonnes, she carried 41 guns and her crew consisted of 140 mariners, 50 soldiers and 20 gunners.

Sir George Beeston rests in Bunbury church, under a semi-circular arch above which is an epitaph recording his career. Consequently, there is some confusion about Sir George Beeston's actual age when he was buried, at Bunbury, on 13 October 1601. George Ormerod in *The History of Cheshire* states unequivocally that his age was 102 and this age has been quoted, almost without exception, ever since. Many dates are not compatible with the career facts stated on Sir George Beeston's epitaph. His age, therefore remains a mystery.

In conclusion, the link between Bunbury's three famous knights is

Bunbury church itself, the stonework of which has remained largely unaltered from medieval times to the present day. Interestingly, both Sir Ralph Egerton and Sir George Beeston would have heard the sound of the present tenor bell, as the bell has never been recast since it was founded in 1510.

John Elsworth

Burleydam

A Century of Schooling at Burleydam

There are a few corners of the Borough of Crewe and Nantwich where the postcode does not start with CW nor is 01270 the telephone area code.

One such place is Burleydam, where both mail and phone calls come via Whitchurch. In addition to being remote, on the edge of borough and county, it is also small, hardly big enough to be termed a village. Nevertheless, it can boast a school building. Nowadays that building offers dancing tuition, but for over a century it was Burleydam Church of England Controlled School, providing a more conventional education for local children. Among these were three generations of my own family.

In the 1950s and '60s, when my sisters and I went to 'Burley-naughty-word', as it was sometimes called, numbers had already fallen to around thirty-five. This foreshadowed the almost inevitable closure a decade later. There were only two classes: infants at the front of the

Burleydam C of E School, the class of 1957-58.

school, juniors at the rear. Moving from one to the other was the only time we had to get accustomed to a new classroom or teacher.

Next door was the Nursery, though it grew plants rather than future pupils. Plant life abounded all around, in fact, as there was open countryside in every other direction; field trips were easily arranged by simply climbing over the back fence. Mr Townsend, the headmaster, taught us much on such 'nature walks' including, on one occasion, the true nature of cuckoo spit. My literal mind found this

hard to take in, and I recall stubbornly arguing that if it was called 'cuckoo spit' then a cuckoo must produce it.

School dinners were not cooked on the premises but arrived each day in large stainless steel containers. They were as good as any other school dinners and I recall taking a particular liking to the custard, even persuading the dinner ladies to let me have a third or fourth helping. It all helped towards my ambition to be the school's weightiest pupil.

As he was self-employed my father was able to take us to school in the car, and

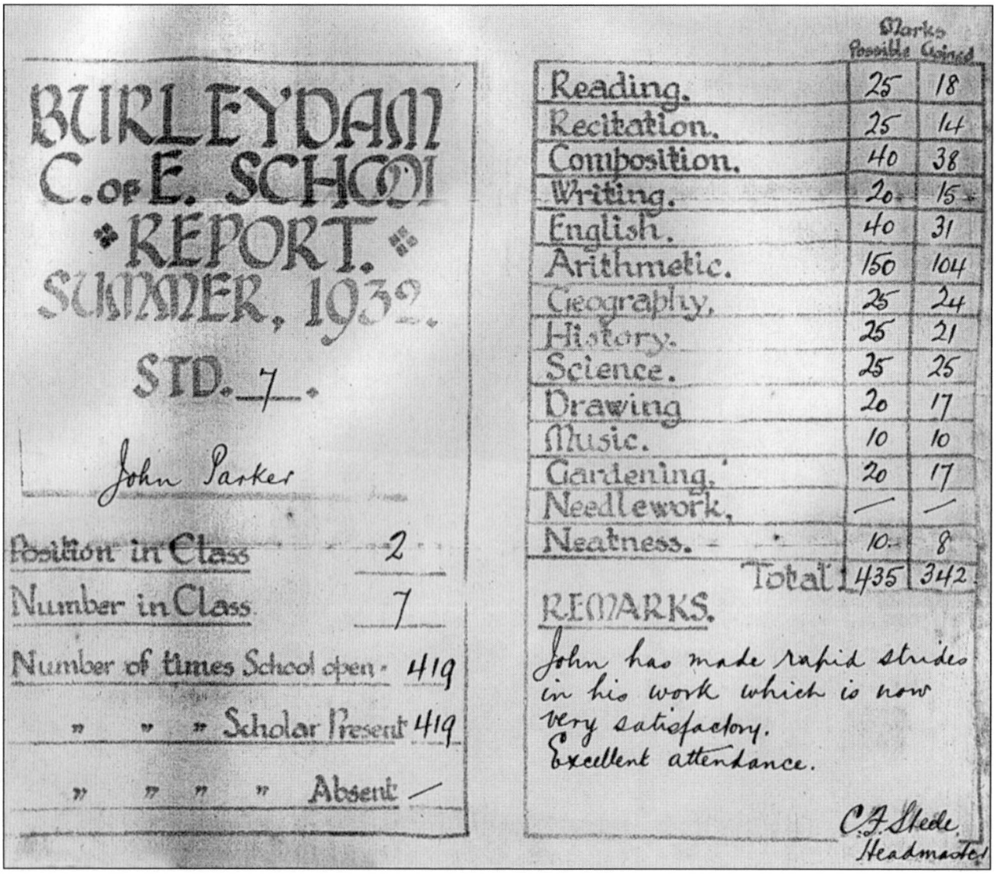

	Marks Possible	Marks Gained
Reading.	25	18
Recitation.	25	14
Composition.	40	38
Writing.	20	15
English.	40	31
Arithmetic.	150	104
Geography.	25	24
History.	25	21
Science.	25	25
Drawing	20	17
Music.	10	10
Gardening.	20	17
Needlework.	—	—
Neatness.	10	8
Total	435	342

BURLEYDAM C. of E. SCHOOL REPORT. SUMMER, 1932.

STD. 7.

John Parker

Position in Class ——— 2

Number in Class ——— 7

Number of times School open · 419

" " " Scholar Present 419

" " " " Absent —

REMARKS.

John has made rapid strides in his work which is now very satisfactory. Excellent attendance.

C.J. Steele
Headmaster

John Parker's school report from 1932.

fetch us home too most days. It was not unusual, though, for him to be unable to leave an urgent job and then we would walk the two miles down Dodds Green Lane to our home at Salesbrook. There were times when snow would fill the lanes and bring us an extra day's holiday. Even in weather such as that, though, we boys would still be wearing shorts; maybe we were hardier then – or fool hardy.

The highlight of the year was the inter-school sports organized by Wrenbury British Legion. These were held on a Saturday in July, in the field opposite the old Salamanca public house at Wrenbury station. Our opponents came from such enormous settlements as Marbury, Cholmondeley and Sound, as well as Wrenbury itself, so the events we managed to win were few and far between. There was a fun fair each year as well, though, so we did not dwell on any disappointing performances in the egg and spoon or sack races. As my father was a member of The Legion we would often be back on the field the next morning, helping to clear up, and even that seemed like fun to us. I remember feeling very hard done to one year when measles confined me to bed while my sisters enjoyed themselves at 'the sports'.

At the age of eleven there was the eleven-plus examination to face and a few months later, depending on how we fared, we had to move on to either Audlem Secondary Modern School or the Grammar School at Nantwich. It was then that we realized just how small a school we had been in.

Back in the 1930s my father, Jack, did not have to face that situation. Not being one of the few to obtain a scholarship to the Grammar School, he continued at Burleydam for his secondary education, up to the age of fourteen.

In the seniors he was taught by the headmaster, Mr Steele, using a room in the centre of the building. Later this was to become the hall, but at that time, with over 100 pupils, there was not enough space for such a luxury. Mr Steele covered most subjects, but Lady Crossly herself would come from Combermere Abbey to take singing. Outside, a large plot was used for gardening lessons, with a considerable quantity of food being produced. Then for half a day each week the seniors would visit the school at Audlem, where there were facilities for the boys to do woodwork and for the girls to learn cookery.

Both my father and his sister were a year late starting school because of fears, later proving to be groundless, that they had weak hearts. Once they did begin their schooling a Scottish doctor who visited the school monitored their condition. The doctor preferred to press his ear firmly against their chests rather than using a stethoscope and his hard head is still impressed on my father's mind.

Until he was old enough to have a bicycle my father's journey to school was undertaken on foot, though there were a number of children to walk with. Occasionally they would catch a ride on George Warburton's coal wagon on its way back to Aston. This was fun and saved a little energy, but was no quicker at all because the horse plodded along at the steadiest of paces. Also, of course, they tended to arrive home as dirty as the coal they had been riding with.

If it were pouring down then my grandfather, William would sometimes give them a lift to school. This was not an option available to most at that time, and neither was it there for William himself when he was a pupil at Burleydam as the nineteenth century ended and the twentieth began. Mr Warner, the school's longest serving headmaster, was in charge then and he provided William with an education perhaps not very different from that later given to my father. However, our specific knowledge of my grandfather's schooldays relates more to extra curricular activities.

The Combermere Arms is only a few yards from the school, and the gamekeeper from the estate found out more than once that it was easily accessible to schoolboys bent on mischief. On emerging from the hostelry to go home he would find his horse and trap still waiting all right, but he could not just ride away. A closer examination revealed that the harness had been undone and then refastened with the horse on one side of the fence and the trap on the other.

My great-grandfather, John, also lived at Salesbrook, but his childhood days fell before the Burleydam school building was erected in 1872. In fact, we have no

A thatched house at Faddiley.

knowledge of what schooling he may have had. One thing we can be sure of, though, is that he did not have to concern himself with learning either postal or telephone codes.

Charles Parker
Prize Winner

Faddiley

Faddiley Folk

Old Tom always had a dew drop at the end of his nose. I remember looking at it shining in the sun and wondering whether he had a fresh one every day or if each one lasted for a few days. He probably held onto it overnight and started a fresh one each morning, was my eventual conclusion.

I remember that Walt had little, sparkly eyes that were generally so screwed up in laughter that I was never able to tell whether he had his eyes open or closed. My childish mind marvelled at how he was able to move around without ever seeming to crash into anything.

And Miss Polly, every day of her life, wore the same long, floral pinny tied in a big bow behind her with matching mobcap on top of her bespectacled head. Her feet were housed in the biggest pair of hob-nailed boots seen this side of a Brighton 'Mods and Rockers' rumble and she rolled from side to side, sailor-like, when she walked, her speed never varying. She always carried a stick – good for indiscriminate poking of cows and people alike and for waving at small children caught scrumping for apples in her orchard. She lived next door to her friend, the pixie-like Wilf who, every year, mowed the grass from his 'long meadows' – grass verges to you and I – and which, when harvested, provided nourishment for his two cows throughout winter.

These people, born and bred in Faddiley, lived in the rural, back lanes of that small parish four miles outside Nantwich, in the middle part of the twentieth century. However, it could have been two centuries earlier – they were as impervious to the world around them changing as they were to the increasing curiosity they were becoming with the passing of each year.

They all lived in smallholdings whose domestic quarters consisted of one up, one down red-brick buildings with a whitewashed loo located outside at the bottom of a black-bricked path. They doubtless all used the same newspaper for the same purpose; probably all rose at dawn and had not one electrical appliance among them. They all spoke in a strange tongue – Tom had a 'Gabriel Archer'-like way of speaking, starting on a high note and winding down to a low whisper; Walt spoke slowly and deliberately but nonetheless unintelligibly, and Miss Polly had a harsh creaky tone with a tendency to snap. This language was apparently 'Broad Cheshire' but it could have been Swahili for the amount most people outside this triumvirate could understand.

Virtually self-sufficient, they each owned a few cows which were faithfully led each day after milking to one of the five or six tiny pastures annexed to each cottage. They all had a handful of poultry, who pecked chirpily around the outbuildings and searched out secret places in which to lay their eggs and, of course, a farm cat. Tom kept a dog. Walt kept rabbits. Miss Polly kept herself to herself.

They were the aboriginal folk of Cheshire, utterly in tune with the earth. Tom encouraged me to watch for the transformation each year of the Pussy Willow from a dull brown, unexciting tree into a glorious Medusa-like froth; he was there on the day I found a four-leaf clover – a coincidental feat which turned him into a magician in my eight-year-old eyes. Walt gave me a rabbit and taught me how to care for the little creature, making me understand that every beating heart, no matter how much fur surrounds it, is attached to a soul. Miss Polly, with her crunching steel-capped boots, out-moded dressing habits and wire-rimmed glasses scared me so much that I could never talk to her. Running away from her in panic one day, I tripped, fell and ripped the skin off my knees. Blinded by my tears and terror, I was hardly aware that the creature crooning strange, squeaky sounds at me as my wounds were gently tended with items plucked from the grasses growing along the lane, was the same person that, seconds ago, I'd been desperate to escape.

I never understood most of what these elderly countryfolk were saying but traditional communication was not needed. I spent a lot of time in their various company and learned to love this land I was living on. Old Tom and Walt, wandering around narrow country lanes with a young girl, were never sources of concern to my mother. I was never snatched away from them in alarm at what they may do to a lone child. The hours spent with these gentle men were semi-silent lessons in the absorption of nature, appreciation of the lives of the flora and fauna of the countryside and an understanding of the live-and-let-live character of the environment.

They are long gone now. Town folk have moved in, razed the smallholdings to the ground and rebuilt them into enormous modern brick country retreats. They have flattened the tiny pastures and hedgerows and converted them into large, ordered gardens, turning natural streams into designer water features. Animals are housed in custom-built stables or kennels and are chosen as much for their sleek appearance as for any practical purpose. After a convenient commute from the city, these born-again countryfolk change into Wellington boots and jackets in

order to pursue their rural activities and I wonder if they ever slow down enough to ponder on the shades of Old Tom, Walt, Wilf and Miss Polly that must surely still inhabit the land and lanes. I like to think I can feel their presence on days when the lanes are lazy with the heat of summer and every creature is going about their business with unhurried movements. When the rhythm of the countryside has pretence of timelessness and unchangeability; and when today's hectic speed is left far behind and replaced by the pace at which the old country folk walked. Quick enough to get things done, but never so fast that the dew drop would tumble.

Dee Reynolds

Haslington

A Day To Remember – A Medal And A Piece Of Cake

The discovery of a small medallion revived a special event that many Crewe people would have remembered until their dying day. It was Saturday afternoon 22 August 1891 and the Mayor and Mayoress of Crewe (Councillor R. Pedley JP and Mrs Pedley) entertained at their residence, Winterley House, on the Crewe-Sandbach road between Haslington and Winterley, the juvenile members of the whole of the Friendly Societies in Crewe and Haslington.

The young people met at their respective lodges at 1 p.m. and marched to the Market Square in Crewe where they boarded twenty lorries. There were upwards of 1,200 children.

The procession departed at 2 p.m. and the strength of the lodges in the procession was as follows:

The Order of Druids: Britannia Lodge 120; Squire Hill 38; Rockwood 134; Brunel 35: Pride of Crewe Lodge 28. The Ancient Order of Foresters 186. The Independent Order of Oddfellows: Loyal Crewe Lodge 129; Strangers' Home Lodge 87; Pride of the Valley Lodge 134. National Independent Order of Oddfellows: Florence Nightingale Lodge 56; Rose of Crewe Lodge 94. Grand United order of Oddfellows: Loyal Pride of Crewe Lodge 42; Perseverance 50; Emblem of Hope 20; Sir Rowland Hill 16; Loyal Excelsior 15. The Independent Order of Rechabites 80. Sons of Temperance 26. Rational Society 4. The Ancient order of Foresters (Haslington) Court Lord Crewe 206.

The procession was accompanied by a detachment of Crewe Borough Police, the Crewe Carriage Works Band and the Crewe Blue Ribbon Band.

The village of Haslington was gaily decorated with flags and an arch across the road. The mayor and mayoress met the procession at the gates of their home, across which was the banner of the Crewe Foresters. The children were escorted to four marquees where they did justice to the viands set before them. Then there were organized sports and a football match between the police and the bandsmen, which the latter won by two goals to one. Up to seventy prizes were presented to competitors.

The mayoress presented between 1,400 and 1,500 medals to the young people and the Mayor decided to present a further 150 medals to those who were detained at home for one reason or another. In order to get some idea of the magnitude of the event the children filed past the Mayoress and received their medals at the rate of about thirty per minute and it took nearly forty minutes to make the distribution. In addition to the medal each child received a packet of cake to eat on the homeward journey.

The mayor Cllr R. Pedley was in business as a Cheese Factor and was also a Baptist Minister. He was locally dubbed 'Dipper' Pedley as he was known to baptize his flock in Winterley Pool (the nearby village pond). Mr Pedley had his own private chapel alongside his home, which can still be seen today.

Brian Edge

Oh For The Simple Life

I still recall life in our cottage as basic but decent.

It was a small cottage, two up, two down, with no hot water or electric light. The toilet was down the bottom of the yard – a brick building, two rooms side by side, so if you heard someone in the next, you kept quiet and very still until they had gone. The 'Night Soil Man' came at about 10.30 p.m. at night in the winter and when it had gone dark in the summer to empty them.

All we had to cook on was the fire and built-in oven next to it, and I remember we had a small Princess stove that was filled with paraffin and lit by putting a light to a small amount of methylated spirits. It was then pumped and it ignited like a gas flame – we used this stove to boil the tin kettle of water or fry food on the top. All other cooking and baking was done in the oven – including baking bread.

We had a tin that had two hooks on which fitted onto the bars of the open fire. Strips of bacon were hung on them and as they cooked the fat fell onto the bottom of the tin, into which we dipped bread – delicious. In the oven there was usually a jar of oats that were cooked in salt water and then made into porridge.

To keep warm in the winter, we had a firebrick that was put into the oven to keep hot, and also an oven shelf, all wrapped up of course, to warm our beds. A candle lit our way upstairs.

We had a lovely brass lamp that hung from the ceiling and was paraffin lit. I was about ten years old when electricity came to Holmes Chapel. It was put in the cottage in only two rooms – one light in the kitchen and one light in one of the bedrooms – it was a few years later that it was put into all four rooms.

Washday was always Monday. The boiler was filled up and the fire lit at 6.30 a.m. The whites were first soaked in soapy water with soda, and then they were boiled, again in soap and soda.

We had no washing powder, just hard soap that was grated and put into the hot water. I remember early powder coming out – Ringo and Hudsons made by Port Sunlight Co. All cotton was always starched, as were collars and cuffs of shirts. All whites were put into a bowl of 'Dolly Blue', this made them whiter.

The washing took all day to do, followed by the cleaning of all floors, which were wet through from all the hot water. Monday night was also always bath night, because the boiler was still hot and full of hot water, until the fire went out, we had a big tin bath, which was filled and put into the back kitchen for us.

I was twenty-three years old and had left home when my mother eventually got hot water and a separate bathroom built.

Nora Schofield